HOW TO DRAW ADVENTURE FRIENDS AND OTHER CARTOON HEROES

BY

CHRIS ALLEN

ROD ESPINOSA AND

DAVID HUTCHISON

ACKNOWLEDGEMENTS
Special thanks to Wes Hartman for his great insights, and to Jamie Billington, Samantha Rodriguez, and Avianna Tiscareño for their suggestions and help.

Book design: Rod Espinosa
Text and Art: Chris Allen, Rod Espinosa, & David Hutchison
Senior editor: Douglas Dlin
Project manager: David Hutchison

First printing, January 2013

ISBN: 978-0-9850925-8-0

Printed and bound in the USA.

Published by Antarctic Press™
7272 Wurzbach Rd. Suite #204
San Antonio, TX, 78240
www.antarctic-press.com

TABLE OF CONTENTS

WHAT YOU'LL NEED TO GET STARTED!

WELCOME TO HOW TO DRAW CARTOON CHARACTERS AND ACTION FRIENDS!

LET'S WARM UP BY DRAWING CIRCLES, TRIANGLES, AND SQUARES. THEY DON'T HAVE TO LOOK LIKE ANYTHING RIGHT AWAY. THIS IS AS MUCH ABOUT WARMING UP OUR MINDS AS IT IS OUR HANDS. AS WE GET USED TO IT, SHAPES WILL START TO FLOW MORE SMOOTHLY, AND THE IMAGES WILL LOOK BETTER BECAUSE OUR HANDS AND MINDS WILL TRULY BE WORKING TOGETHER!

IF YOU'RE LOOKING FOR EXTRA IDEAS, BE SURE TO CHECK OUT THE TIP BOXES ON THE SIDES OF PAGES LATER IN THE BOOK!

BASIC CHARACTER SHAPES

NOW LET'S TRY DRAWING PEOPLE WITH THE SQUARES, TRIANGLES, AND CIRCLES WE'VE BEEN PRACTICING WITH. WHAT KIND OF BODY TYPES DO THEY SUGGEST TO YOU? TALL? SHORT? SKINNY? MAYBE A BODY BUILDER OR A SUMO WRESTLER?

BASIC CHARACTER SHAPES

LET'S GO AHEAD AND START CREATING SOME CHARACTERS USING THE SHAPES WE'VE BEEN SKETCHING. WE'LL START WITH CIRCLES, SINCE THEY ARE THE SIMPLEST AND MOST NATURAL FOR BEGINNERS.

1) THIS MAIN CIRCLE IS WHAT WE'LL BASE THE REST OF THE CHARACTER ON.

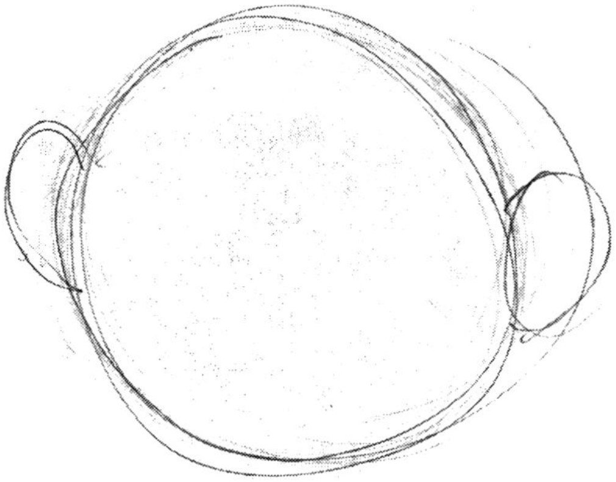

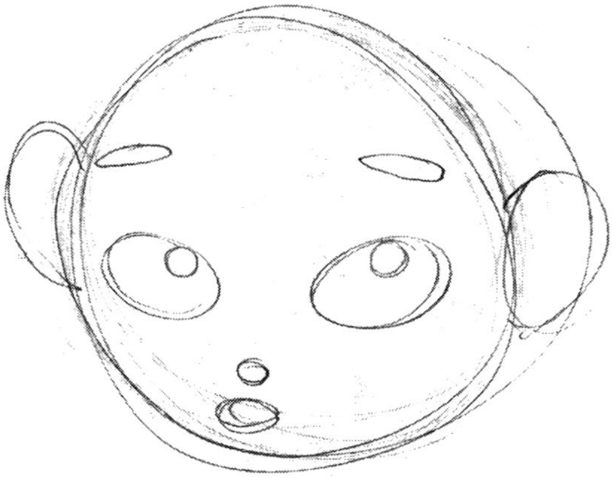

2) WHERE WE PLACE THE EYES, NOSE, AND MOUTH CAN HAVE A HUGE EFFECT ON THE FINAL LOOK OF OUR CHARACTER. IF WE MAKE A MISTAKE, WE CAN ALWAYS ERASE.

3) WE'LL MAKE THE HAIR CURLY, JUST TO KEEP WITH THE THEME OF CIRCLES.

TRY DRAWING CIRCLES USING YOUR WHOLE ARM. RESTING YOUR WRIST AND ELBOW ON THE TABLE CAN KEEP THE LINES YOU DRAW FROM LOOKING SMOOTH.

4) IF WE WANT TO INK OUR ART, WE NEED TO FIND THE RIGHT KIND OF PEN. TESTING DIFFERENT TYPES OF PENS TO FIND OUT WHICH WORK BEST IS IMPORTANT!

5) HERE WE GO! NOT BAD FOR A FIRST TRY. IF WE KEEP PRACTICING, OUR CHARACTERS WILL START LOOKING BETTER IN NO TIME.

FLIP THE SCRIPT!

HERE'S A COOL LITTLE EXPERIMENT WE CAN DO. WE'VE MADE A CHARACTER, BUT IS THIS AS FAR AS WE CAN GO? LET'S FLIP THE SCRIPT AND TURN OUR DESIGN ON ITS HEAD!

NOW LET'S TRY TO MAKE A NEW CHARACTER BASED ON OUR UPSIDE-DOWN GUY!

OKAY, THAT'S PRETTY FUNNY!

BASIC CHARACTER SHAPES

WE'VE TRIED OUT CIRCLES, SO HOW ABOUT A HEAD MADE WITH JUST TRIANGLES? WE'RE USING SIMPLE SHAPES, BUT THAT DOESN'T MEAN IT WILL BE EASY!

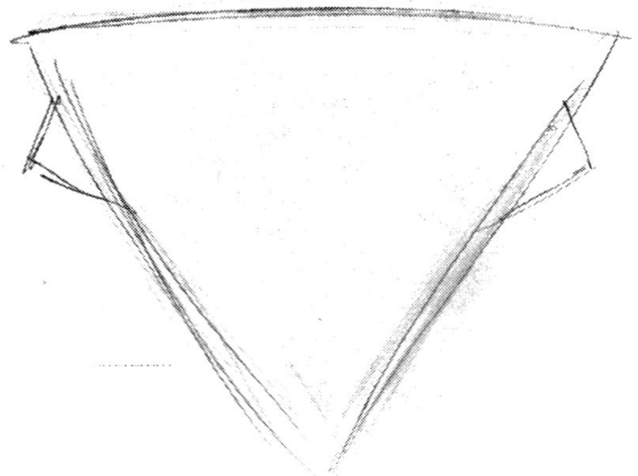

1) HERE'S OUR BASIC HEAD WITH EARS. NOW LET'S WORK ON THE FACE.

2) CREATING A FACE JUST FROM TRIANGLES CAN BE DIFFICULT, BECAUSE YOU NEED TO ARRANGE THE SHAPES SO THAT THE FACE LOOKS GOOD.

3) LET'S FINISH BY ADDING HAIR. THE HIGH COLLAR KEEPS OUR EYE FROM BEING DRAWN TO THE BOTTOM OF THE PICTURE.

4) HERE'S THE FINAL DRAWING. THIS IS AN INTERESTING EXPERIMENT, BUT WE'LL NEED MORE PRACTICE TO REALLY PULL THIS OFF!

5) LET'S DO ANOTHER TRIANGLE-BASED HEAD, BUT WHY DON'T WE MIX IN SOME OTHER SHAPES TO BALANCE THE DRAWING OUT A LITTLE BETTER?

HERE'S OUR TRIANGLE, SO WHAT CAN WE DO TO CHANGE UP THE DESIGN?

6) LET'S ADD SOME CIRCULAR SHAPES TO MAKE THE DESIGN A LITTLE MORE CARTOONY AND LESS STALE.

7) THAT'S BETTER! WE NEED TO DO THESE KINDS OF EXPERIMENTS IF WE'RE GOING TO FIND OUR OWN STYLE.

1) WHEN WOULD WE WANT TO USE SQUARES? THEY'RE MOSTLY FOR HEAVYSET FOLKS OR GUYS WE NEED TO HAVE A TRULY SQUARE JAW.

TRY TO DRAW YOUR SQUARES BY HAND. MAKING YOUR SQUARES TOO PERFECT CAN MAKE THEM LOOK STIFF AND BORING.

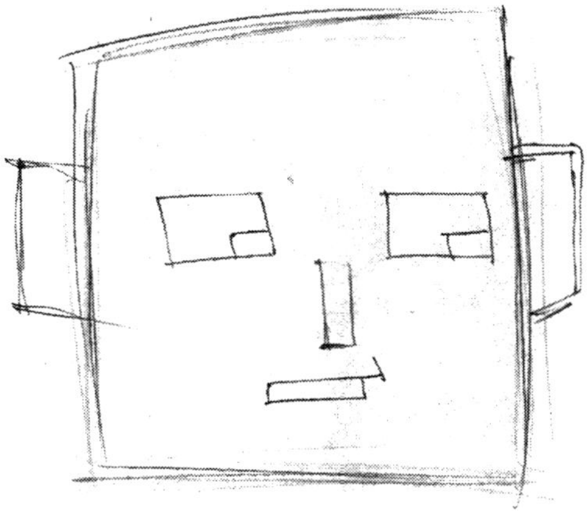

2) AS WITH THE OTHER EXAMPLES, WE'LL TRY TO USE SQUARE SHAPES TO REPRESENT THE EYES, NOSE, AND MOUTH.

3) YEP, EVEN THE HAIR IS GOING TO BE MADE UP OF SQUARES!

IN THE FINAL DRAWING, BUMPING THE CHIN OUT A BIT HELPED GIVE OUR CHARACTER A LITTLE MORE...WELL, CHARACTER!

REMEMBER, JUST A FEW SLIGHT CHANGES CAN CREATE A TOTALLY DIFFERENT TYPE OF IMAGE! ADJUSTING PARTS OF THE FACE AND SHRINKING OR ENLARGING SOME PARTS MAKE THIS GUY SEEM A LOT MORE AGGRESSIVE.

WHY DON'T WE TRY DRAWING SOME ANIMALS USING SOME OF THE SKILLS WE'VE PRACTICED? THE SHAPE OF A CAT'S HEAD IS A LOT LIKE A TRIANGLE TO SOME FOLKS, SO LET'S SEE HOW WELL THAT WORKS!

NOT BAD! LET'S MAKE UP A POSE THAT HAS A LITTLE MORE ACTION TO IT!

1) IT'S THE SAME IDEA FOR THIS DRAWING, BUT WE'RE GOING TO MAKE OUR CAT A LITTLE MORE LIVELY!

2) AGAIN, WE'VE BASED AS MUCH OF THE DESIGN ON TRIANGLES AS POSSIBLE. MAYBE OUR CAT NEEDS A LITTLE FRIEND?

3) NOW HE'S HAVING FUN!

YOU KNOW WHAT? I SEE SOMETHING ELSE WE CAN DO WITH THIS DRAWING. IT'S TIME TO **FLIP THE SCRIPT!**

FLIP THE SCRIPT!

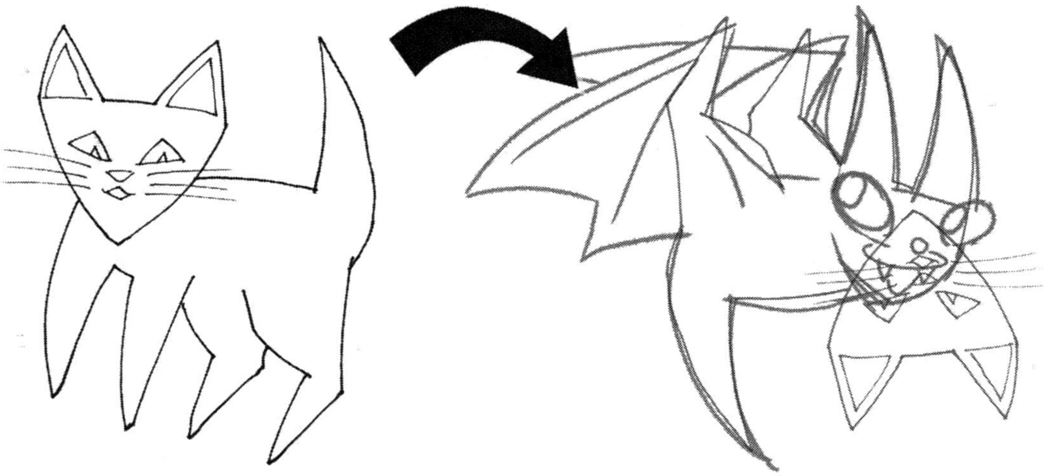

INTERESTING...THERE WAS A BAT HIDING IN THAT CAT DRAWING!

VISUAL VOCABULARY

THERE'S MORE TO CARTOONING THAN JUST BEING ABLE TO DRAW A CHARACTER. YOU NEED TO BRING THEM TO LIFE! ADDING TO YOUR VISUAL VOCABULARY CAN GO A LONG WAY TOWARD MAKING YOUR CHARACTERS MORE FUN AND LIVELY!

1

VEAT:
S HELPS US SHOW
RSON IS UNDER
T STRESS.

2

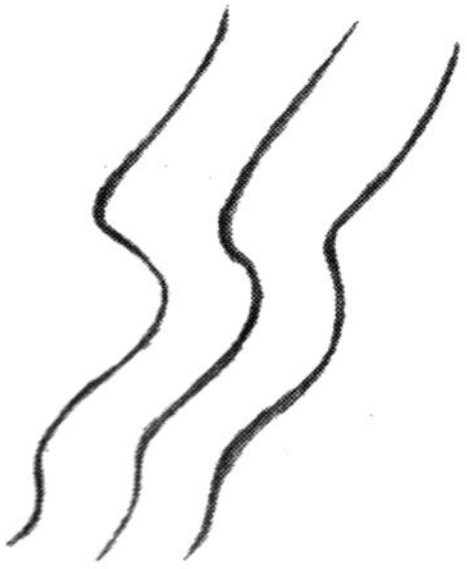

SMOKE:
WE CAN ALSO USE THIS TO SHOW STEAM OR A BAD SMELL.

3

SWING:
USED FOR SOMEONE THROWING A PUNCH OR SWINGING A BAT.

W
SON

5

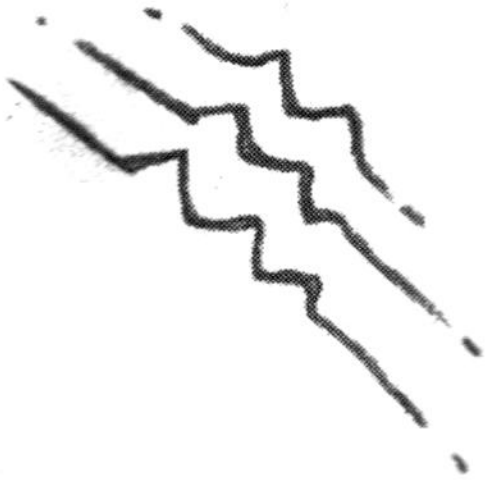

SHIVER:
TO SHOW SOMEONE IS COLD OR SCARED!

6

WIGGLE:
GOOD FOR SHOWING BODY PARTS MOVING OR JIGGLING.

LET'S DRAW ANOTHER CHARACTER--NOT JUST A HEAD, BUT A FULL BODY. BUILDING THE BODY USING CIRCLES AND OVALS IS USUALLY THE SIMPLEST WAY OF DOING IT.

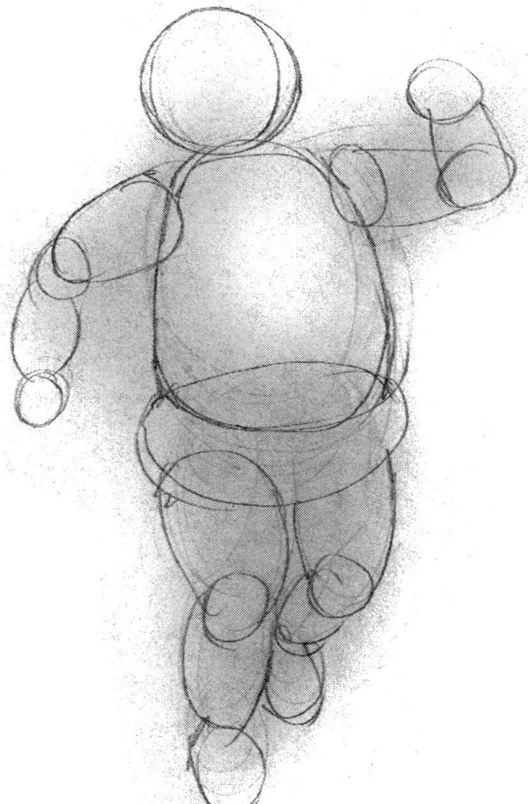

1) THIS MAY NOT LOOK VERY SIMPLE AT FIRST, BUT AS WE GET USED TO STARTING DRAWING LIKE THIS, WE'LL BE ABLE TO DO IT WITHOUT THINKING.

2) ONCE WE'VE SKETCHED OUT THE BODY, WE CAN DRAW THE ACTUAL CHARACTER OVER IT.

3) HERE'S THE FINISHED DRAWING. THE POLKA DOT PATTERN ON OUR CHARACTER'S SHIRT IS THERE TO HELP LIVEN UP THE DRAWING A LITTLE.

4) HERE, THE HAIR AND PANTS HAVE BEEN FILLED IN WITH BLACK. THE CONTRAST CAN REALLY HELP THE FIGURE POP OFF OF THE PAGE!

SINCE WE'VE ALREADY TALKED ABOUT SOME OF THE WAYS WE CAN IMPROVE OUR CARTOONS BY ADDING EXTRA VISUAL ELEMENTS, LET'S TRY A FEW OF THEM ON THIS DRAWING!

LITTLE TOUCHES LIKE THESE MAKE IT CLEAR THAT OUR CHARACTER IS RUNNING AND REALLY GIVING IT HER ALL!

BASIC CHARACTER SHAPES

DRAWING A FULL CHARACTER CAN BE HARD IF YOU AREN'T SURE WHAT IT IS YOU'RE GOING TO DRAW. TRY TO IMAGINE A SCENE IN YOUR HEAD BEFORE PUTTING PENCIL TO PAPER.

1) ONCE WE HAVE A STRONG IMAGE IN MIND, WE CAN MORE EASILY BEGIN PUTTING DOWN THE BASIC SHAPES WE'LL NEED TO DRAW THE CHARACTER.

2) ONCE THAT'S DONE, WE CAN SKETCH IN THE FACE AND CLOTHES WE WANT FOR THE CHARACTER. NOW IS ALSO A GOOD TIME FOR US TO ADD ANY PROPS THE CHARACTER MIGHT HAVE.

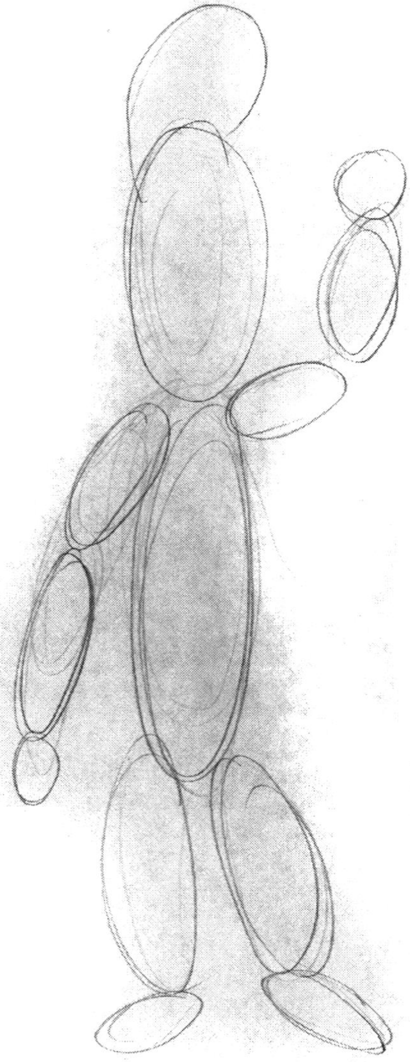

3) TRY TO KEEP YOUR DESIGN SIMPLE. OFTEN, A DRAWING CAN BECOME CLUTTERED WITH DETAIL AND UNNECESSARY LINES EVERYWHERE. BEING CLEAR AND DIRECT IS THE BEST POLICY IN CARTOONING!

WHY DO CARTOON CHARACTERS HAVE FOUR FINGERS?

WELL, BECAUSE IT'S EASIER AND FASTER TO DRAW. MOST OF THE TIME, PEOPLE LOOKING AT THE DRAWING WON'T EVEN NOTICE!

LET'S DRAW A BOY AND HIS DOG. WE CAN GET TWO CHARACTERS FOR THE PRICE OF ONE!

1) WE'LL START BY BUILDING OUR CHARACTERS USING THE SHAPES WE'VE ALREADY PRACTICED WITH. IT'S BEST TO DRAW THE WHOLE FIGURE, EVEN IF YOUR CHARACTERS OVERLAP.

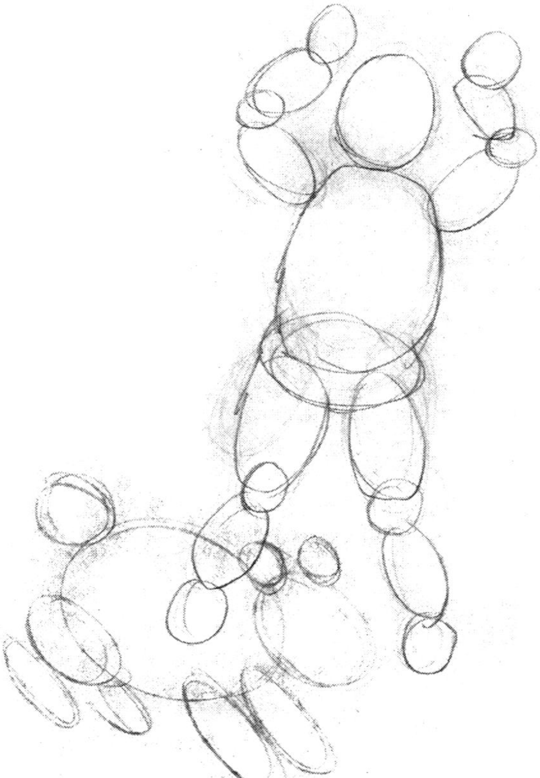

2) FROM THERE, WE NEED TO FLESH OUT THE BOY AND DOG. I CAN'T TELL YOU THE BREED OF THE DOG. HE MAY BE ALIEN IN ORIGIN!

3) FOR THE FINISHED DRAWING, ADDING AN ICE CREAM CONE HELPS BALANCE OUT THE PICTURE AND MAKES THE BOY'S SURPRISE EASIER TO UNDERSTAND.

LET'S DO ONE LAST EXAMPLE FOR FIGURES USING OVALS.

1) AS YOU CAN SEE, THIS COMES CLOSEST TO THE STANDARD FIGURE THAT WE'VE DONE.

2) ONCE THE FRAME IS ESTABLISHED, WE CAN THEN PUT IN THE FINER WORK OF FACIAL DETAILS, AS WELL AS CLOTHING. NOTICE WE ALSO USED CIRCLES FOR HER HAIR AND SLEEVES.

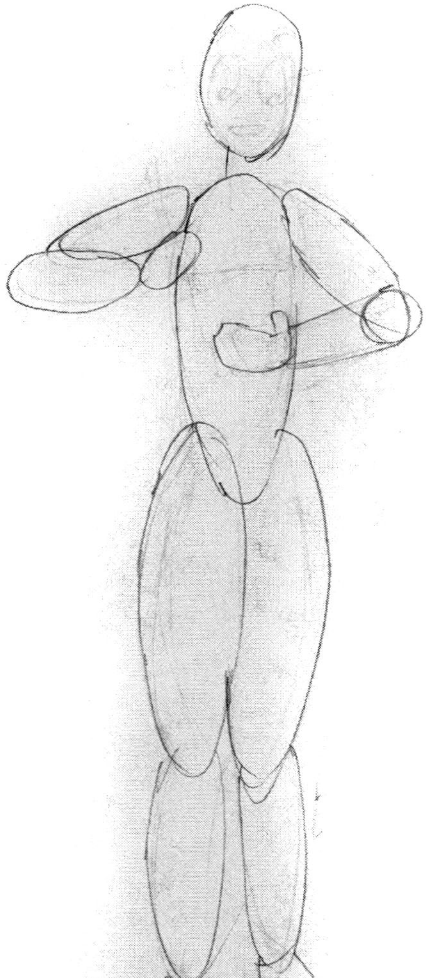

3) IT WAS FUN DRAWING THIS ONE. I THINK THE BEST PART WAS COMING UP WITH THE LOOK ON THIS LADY'S FACE!

OUR NEXT PRACTICE INVOLVES SQUARE AND RECTANGULAR SHAPES. RECTANGLES ARE PERFECT FOR DEPICTING TALL OR SKINNY CHARACTERS, SO LET'S GO DRAW A WORKING MAN REALLY QUICKLY.

1) WE'LL BEGIN BY DRAWING RECTANGLES FOR THE HEAD, BODY, AND LIMBS.

2) NEXT, WE NEED TO NAIL DOWN THE WORKER'S FACE AND THE KIND OF CLOTHING WE WANT HIM TO WEAR.

HERE'S OUR FINISHED DRAWING. NOT BAD, BUT SOMETHING FEELS OFF. OUR CHARACTER JUST DOESN'T SEEM TO BE PUTTING MUCH EFFORT INTO CATCHING THAT BUS. MAYBE THERE'S A WAY WE CAN PUT SOME PEP INTO HIS STEP?

THAT'S MORE LIKE IT! BY SHIFTING THE CHARACTER'S BODY FORWARD, WE MAKE IT SEEM AS IF HE'S REALLY RUSHING AHEAD. SPEEDLINES ALSO ADD TO THE SENSE OF MOTION!

SQUARES ARE ALSO GREAT FOR DEPICTING STOCKY PEOPLE OR SMALL CHILDREN. LET'S DO A COUPLE HERE.

USING THESE BLOCKY SHAPES CAN MAKE CREATING CHARACTERS QUICK AND EASY, SINCE THEY MAKE FOR GREAT BODY TYPES AND FILL UP A LOT OF SPACE.

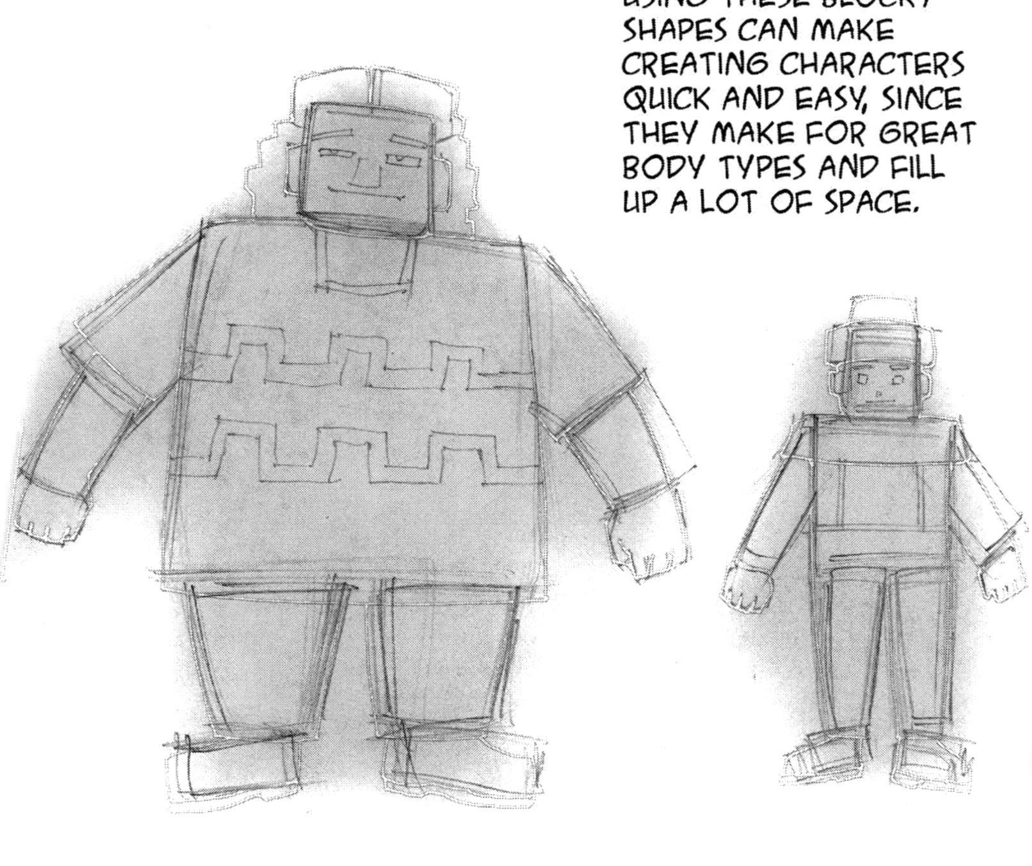

OUR BIG GUY LOOKS...KIND OF BIG. AT LEAST, HE LOOKS LARGER THAN THE OTHER GUY. OR IS THE BIG GUY JUST A LOT CLOSER TO US? IS THERE ANY WAY TO MAKE IT CLEAR JUST HOW LARGE EACH OF THESE CHARACTERS ARE?

TO MAKE OUR BIG GUY SEEM EVEN MORE HUGE, LET'S PLACE THE SMALL GUY IN FRONT OF HIM.

FINALLY, LET US REVISIT THE TRIANGLE! YOU MAY THINK IT'S HARD TO CREATE A HUMAN FIGURE OUT OF ALL TRIANGLES, BUT ONCE WE'VE HAD SOME PRACTICE, IT REALLY ISN'T A PROBLEM. LET'S DRAW!

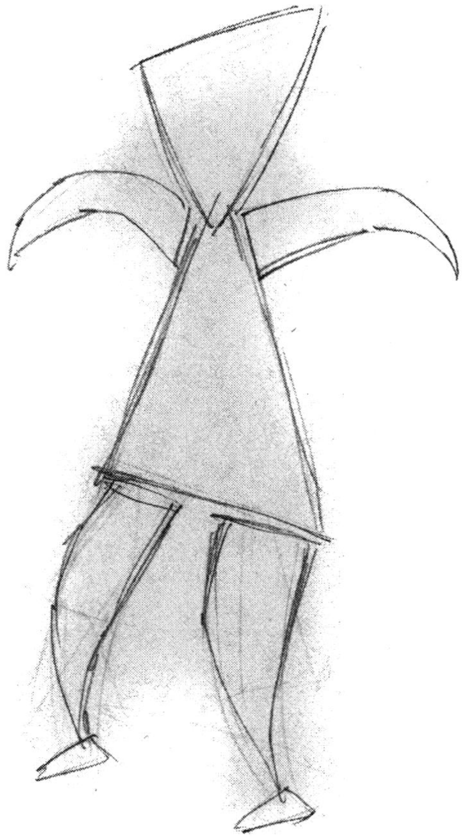

1) THERE'S NO RULE THAT SAYS WE CAN'T BEND OUR TRIANGLES, SO LET'S DO THAT HERE. THIS WILL GIVE US A LITTLE FLEXIBILITY IN MAKING OUR FIGURE.

2) ONCE WE'VE GOT THE POSE RIGHT, WE CAN ADD IN DETAILS SUCH AS THE FACE, HAIR, CLOTHES AND SURFBOARD. NOTICE THE HAIR IS ALSO MADE OF TRIANGLES. THIS IS USUALLY MEANT FOR MORE WILD AND ADVENTUROUS CHARACTERS.

3) WE FILL IN THE BLACK AREAS OF HER HAIR AND HER WETSUIT. THIS MAKES SUCH A HUGE DIFFERENCE AND HELPS HER FIGURE TO POP OUT MORE.

PRETTY COOL! STILL, I THINK THERE'S SOMETHING ELSE WE CAN DO HERE. IT'S TIME TO FLIP THE SCRIPT AGAIN!

FLIP THE SCRIPT!

WOW! THIS IS OUR CRAZIEST DESIGN YET! THERE AREN'T MANY THINGS THAT CAN TOP THAT MUSTACHE! WHAT WOULD YOU DO? I HOPE YOU'LL TRY YOUR HAND AT THIS, AS THE RESULTS CAN BE PRETTY SHOCKING!

LET'S DRAW ANOTHER TRIANGLE LADY. WE'LL KEEP WITH OUR SIMPLIFIED THEME A BIT LONGER BEFORE WE GO INTO MORE COMPLICATED DESIGNS.

1) THIS IS A GOOD CASE FOR USING TRIANGLES, BECAUSE IT'S CLEAR THAT YOU CAN GET A FEEL FOR THE TYPE OF CHARACTER WE'RE DRAWING ALMOST AT ONCE!

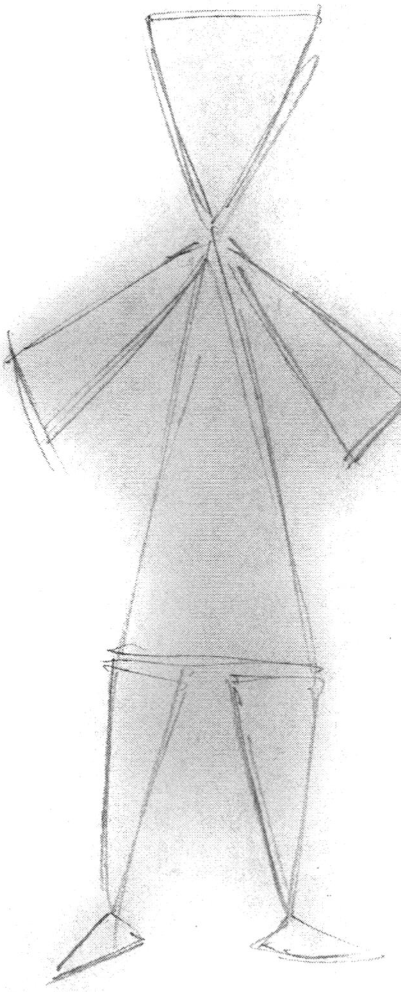

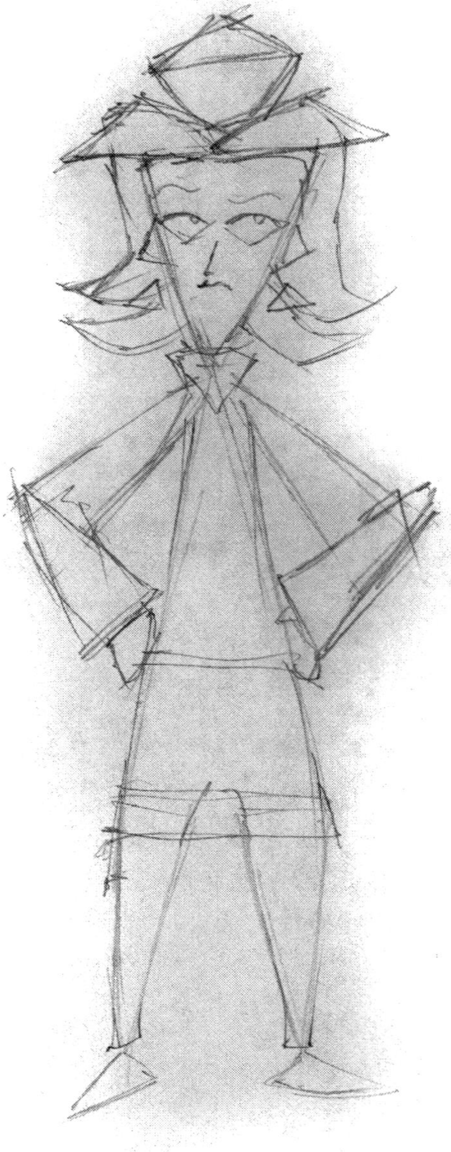

HERE, WE'LL ADD ANOTHER PAIR OF TRIANGLES TO HER ARMS, MORE TRIANGLES TO MAKE HER HAIR, AND TRIANGLES TO MAKE HER FACE. THERE ARE TRIANGLES EVERYWHERE--THIS IS GETTING OUT OF HAND!

3) ANOTHER GOOD THING ABOUT CREATING A CHARACTER THIS WAY IS HOW STRONG THE OUTLINE IS. SQUINT YOUR EYES, AND YOU'LL SEE WHAT I'M TALKING ABOUT!

OF COURSE, TRIANGLES LEND THEMSELVES TO ALL KINDS OF BODY TYPES. LET'S EXPLORE ONE MORE BEFORE WE MOVE ON.

1) HAVING CREATED SIMILAR FIGURES SO MANY TIMES ALREADY, THIS SHOULD BE SECOND NATURE BY NOW! WITH OUR BASIC FIGURE DONE, WE CAN MOVE ON TO ADDING MAJOR ELEMENTS SUCH AS THE DESIGN OF THE FACE, THE TRACK SUIT, AND ANY PROPS, LIKE THE DUMBBELL.

2) THE FINISHING TOUCHES FOR THIS DRAWING WERE THE SWEAT DROPS AND SOME MOTION LINES TO SHOW JUST HOW HARD OUR FITNESS EXPERT IS WORKING OUT!

VISUAL VOCABULARY

IF YOU LOOK AT MANY OF THE CONSTRUCTION DRAWINGS FOR CARTOON CHARACTERS, YOU'LL SEE CROSSHAIRS LIKE THESE ON THEIR HEADS AND BODIES. WHY? IF AN ARTIST IS CREATING A CHARACTER ON THE FLY, FOR THE FIRST TIME, THEY PROBABLY WON'T USE THESE CROSSHAIRS.

OFTEN, THESE ARE USED BY CARTOONISTS AND ANIMATORS AS A QUICK AND CONVENIENT WAY OF CENTERING AND LINING UP THE FEATURES OF A CHARACTER'S FACE AS WELL AS THE CENTER LINE OF A CHARACTERS BODY. THEY NEED THESE LINES SO THAT THEY CAN DRAW THE SAME CHARACTER OVER AND OVER AGAIN AND KEEP THEM LOOKING THE SAME FROM PANEL TO PANEL, PAGE TO PAGE. MAKING A CHARACTER LOOK CONSISTENT IS VITAL TO AN ANIMATOR, WHOSE CHARACTERS NEED TO LOOK RIGHT WHILE IN MOTION, FROM ANY ANGLE!

WORKING WITH SOFT SHAPES!

THIS IS WHERE DRILLING THOSE SHAPES INTO OUR HEADS STARTS TO PAY OFF. WE WANT TO BE ABLE TO CALL ON THOSE BASIC SHAPES ALMOST ON INSTINCT WHEN WE'RE CREATING CHARACTERS.

BEING ABLE TO SHIFT FORMS AND PLAY AROUND WITH HOW OUR CHARACTERS' EYES, NOSES AND MOUTHS FIT TOGETHER WILL GIVE US MORE VARIETY IN OUR DESIGNS, AND PROVIDE US SOME UNIQUE CHARACTERS.

I CALL THESE "SOFT SHAPES" BECAUSE THEY AREN'T AS RIGID AND CONTROLLED AS SOME OF THE DESIGNS WE WERE WORKING ON BEFORE. ALSO, THESE CHARACTER FEATURE MORE ROUNDED SHAPES NO MATTER WHAT BASIC SHAPES WERE USED THE BUILD THEM.

HOPEFULLY, THESE DRAWINGS WILL GIVE YOU AN IDEA OF WHERE YOU CAN TAKE YOUR OWN WORK!

CARTOON CHARACTERS AND THE LINE OF ACTION!

IS THERE ANYTHING MORE PATHETIC THAN A STATIC CARTOON CHARACTER? JUST STANDING THERE, STRAIGHT AS A FENCE POST. GOING NOWHERE AND NOT REALLY DOING ANYTHING WORTH PAYING ATTENTION TO...*BORING.* LUCKILY, CARTOONISTS HAVE A CURE FOR THIS CONDITION: IT'S CALLED THE LINE OF ACTION!

THE LINE OF ACTION IS A SIMPLE GUIDELINE THAT CAN IMPROVE ANY POSE INSTANTLY!

GENERALLY, ARTISTS USE THE LINE OF ACTION AS A SPINE TO BUILD THEIR CHARACTERS ON, BUT IT'S BEST USED FOR CHARACTERS IN MOTION. PUNCHING, JUMPING, AND KICKING ALL BECOME EASIER TO SHOW IF YOU USE THE LINE OF MOTION TO GUIDE YOU!

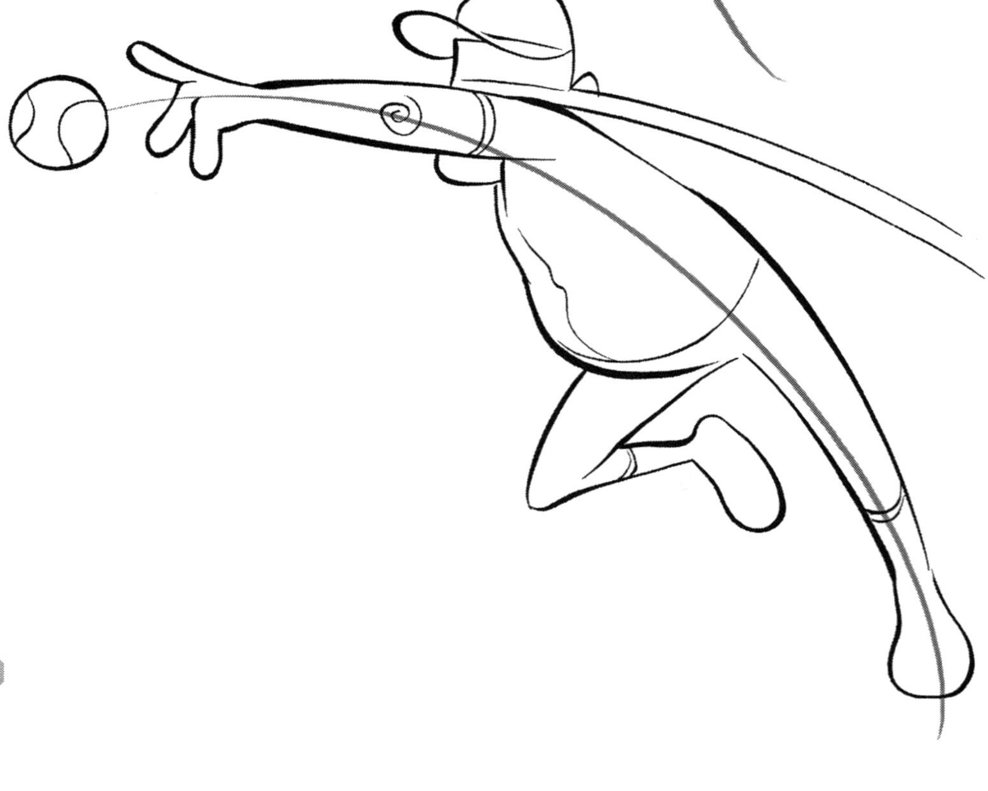

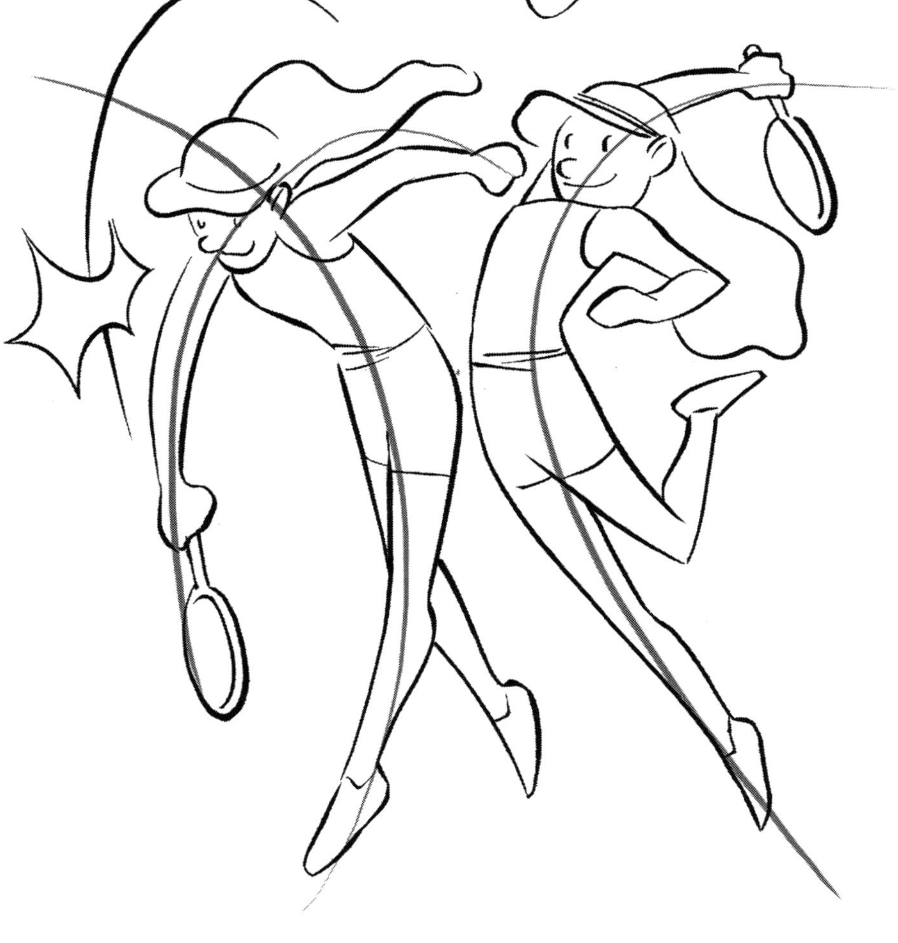

THE LINE OF ACTION IS ALSO GREAT FOR SUPER-HEROIC CHARACTERS! I CAN'T THINK OF POSE THAT WOULDN'T BENEFIT FROM THIS GUIDELINE. TRY IT OUT IN YOUR OWN WORK. YOU'LL BE GLAD YOU DID!

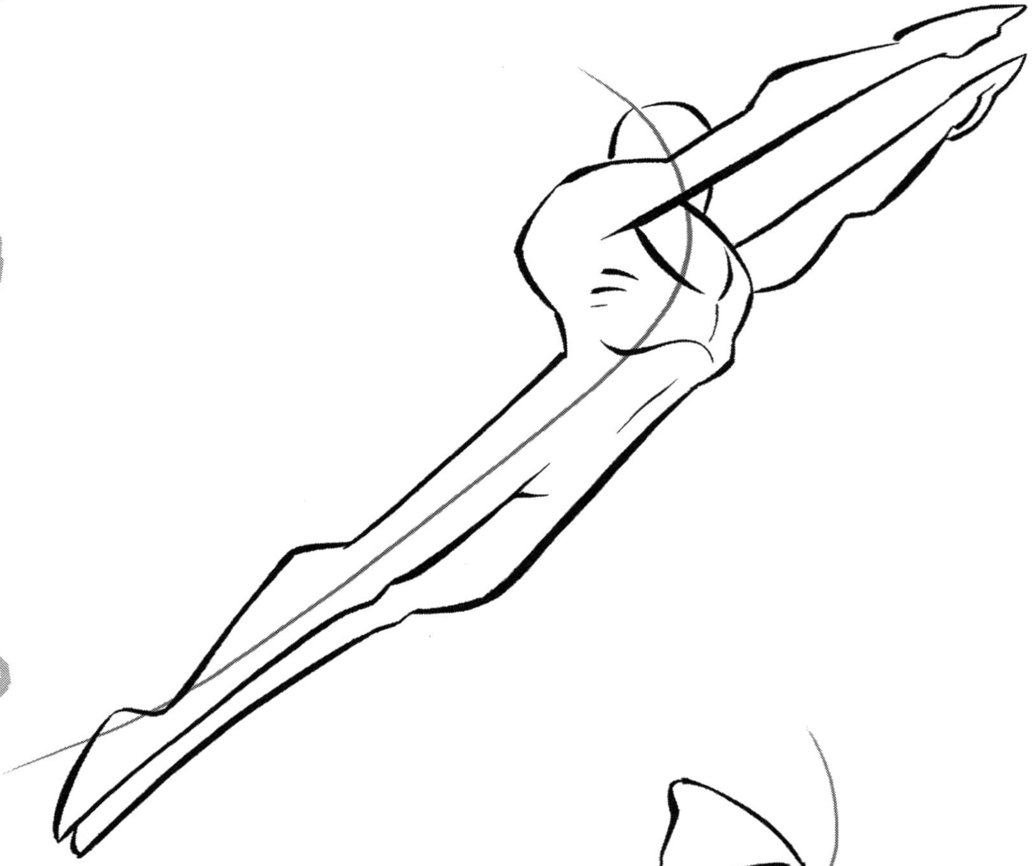

VISUAL VOCABULARY

WHAT ARE WE TALKING ABOUT WHEN WE SAY "FOREGROUND", "MIDGROUND", AND "BACKGROUND"?

MOST PICTURES HAVE EACH OF THESE ELEMENTS. SIMPLY PUT, THE FOREGROUND CONTAINS ANY OBJECTS THAT ARE CLOSEST TO US. THE MIDGROUND IS USUALLY WHERE THE CHARACTERS ARE IN THE DRAWING. THE BACKGROUND IS FOR ANYTHING THAT IS FARTHER AWAY FROM US, LIKE CITIES, MOUNTAINS, AND THE SKY.

DO YOU HAVE A HEAD FOR CARTOONING?

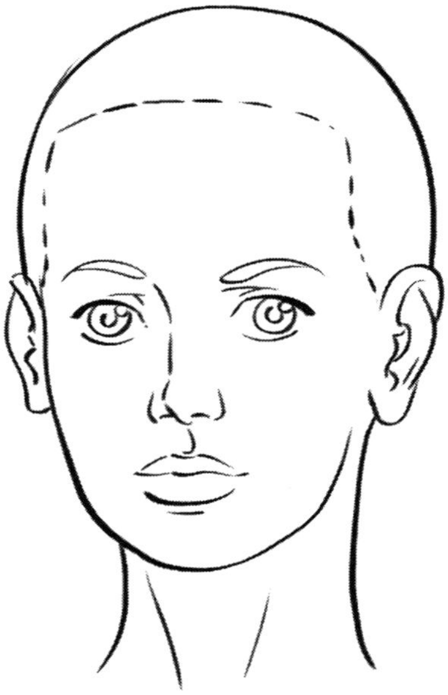

IF WE'RE GOING TO BE BETTER CARTOONISTS, KNOWING THE LANDMARKS OF THE FACE AND HOW THEY RELATE CAN BE A BIG HELP.

LET'S TAKE A LOOK AT THE HEAD AND SEE SOME OF THE WAYS IT CAN BE EXAGGERATED TO COMIC EFFECT.

IN GENERAL, WE WANT TO GIVE A GIRLS' HEADS MORE CURVED AND FLOWING SHAPES TO MAKE IT CLEAR THAT THEY'RE, YOU KNOW, GIRLS.

1) HERE WE GAVE THE GIRL A BIGGER CHEEK THAN NORMAL. THIS IS GOOD FOR YOUNGER CHARACTERS.

2) HERE THE HEAD IS LONGER AND A LITTLE MORE ANGULAR. BEST USED FOR ADULTS.

3) THIS HEAD USES PARTS FROM HEADS ONE AND TWO. GOOD FOR DRAWING TEENAGERS.

4) THIS WORKS WELL FOR CHARACTERS WITH A CERTAIN STYLE. YOU'LL SEE A LOT OF ALIEN CHARACTERS WITH THIS HEAD SHAPE.

FOR COMPARISON

OKAY, BUT WHAT ABOUT THE GUYS? HERE ARE SOME MORE EXAMPLES FOR US TO THINK ABOUT!

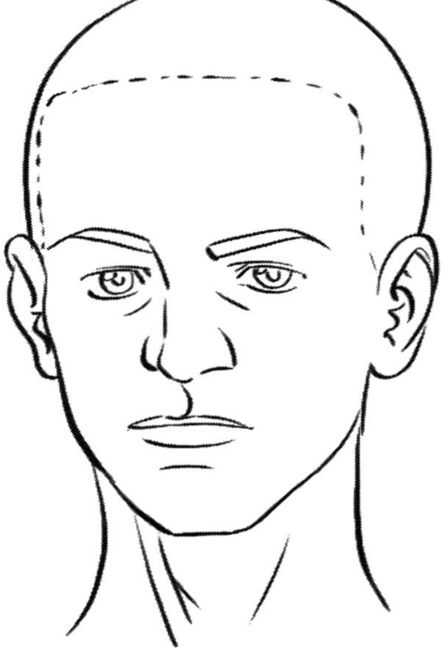

SOME COMMON ELEMENTS TO REMEMBER FOR DRAWING BOYS ARE A HEAVIER BROW, A LARGER NOSE, AND A STRONGER CHIN. THESE ARE JUST GENERAL GUIDELINES, AND IT REALLY DEPENDS ON THE KIND OF CHARACTER WE'RE CREATING.

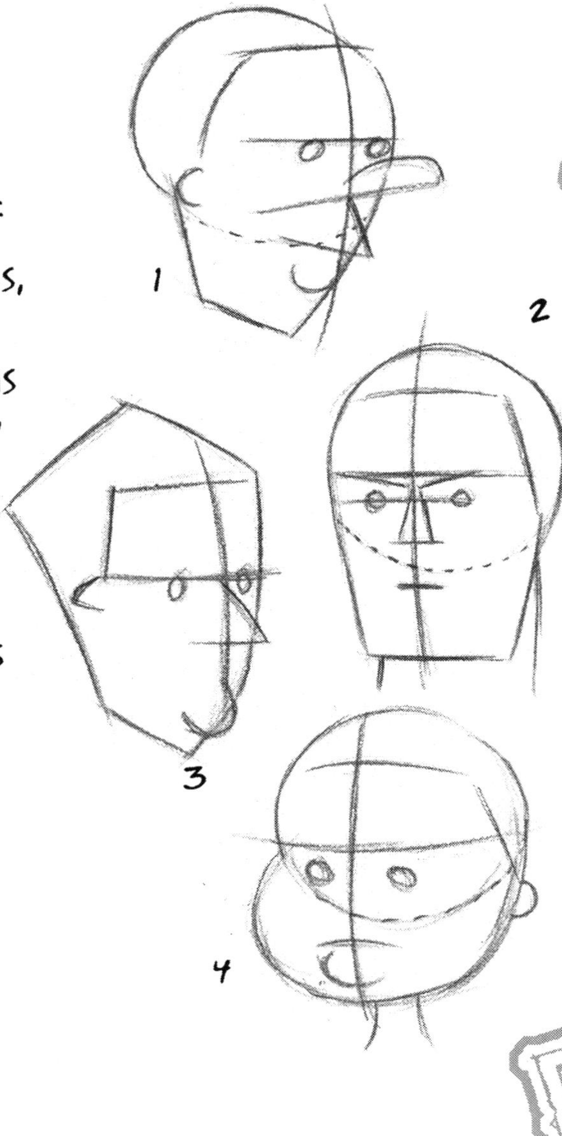

1) HERE THE CHIN AND NECK KIND OF BLEND TOGETHER. THIS MAKES THE CHIN SEEM WEAKER. IN SOME DESIGNS, THE CHIN IS REMOVED ALTOGETHER.

2) WE HAVE A CONSTRUCTION THAT IS MUCH CLOSER TO THE CLASSIC STYLE, BUT THE DISTANCE BETWEEN THE MOUTH AND CHIN IS GREATER.

3) WE START BY USING A FREEHAND GEOMETRIC SHAPE.

4) WE SET THE HAIR AND BROW LINES IN, AND THEN DRAW A SIMPLIFIED, ROUNDED JAWLINE OFF OF THE CIRCLE OF THE CRANIUM.

FOR COMPARISON

NOW LET'S COMPARE SOME CARTOON WOMEN WITH A MORE REALISTIC FIGURE.

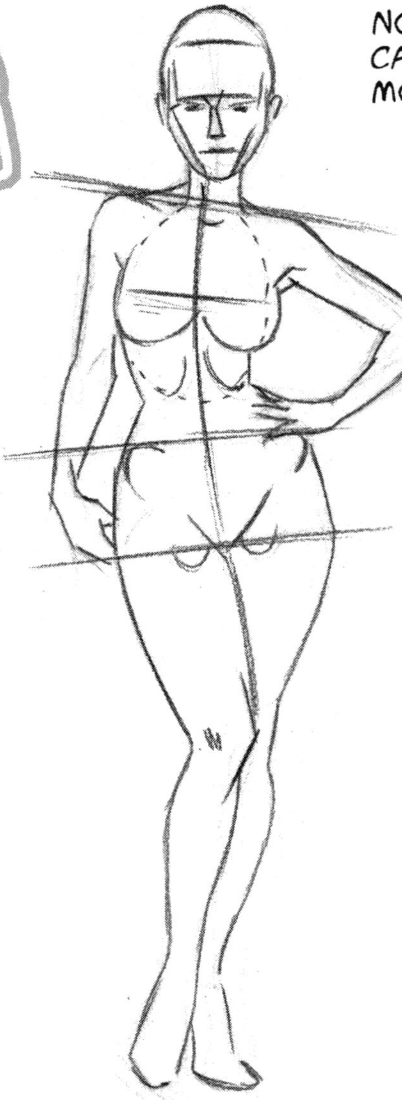

1) WE ARE USING THE CURVES OF THE TORSO AND THE HIPS TO EMPHASIZE THE HOURGLASS FIGURE.

2) WE ARE STILL DRAWING A KIND OF HOURGLASS, BUT OUR FIGURE IS CONSTRUCTED WITH ALMOST ALL STRAIGHT LINES.

3) WE ARE EMPHASIZING THE HIPS BY MAKING THEM MUCH WIDER THAN THE SHOULDERS, WHILE STILL KEEPING THE LIMBS TAPERED AND THE HANDS AND FEET SMALL.

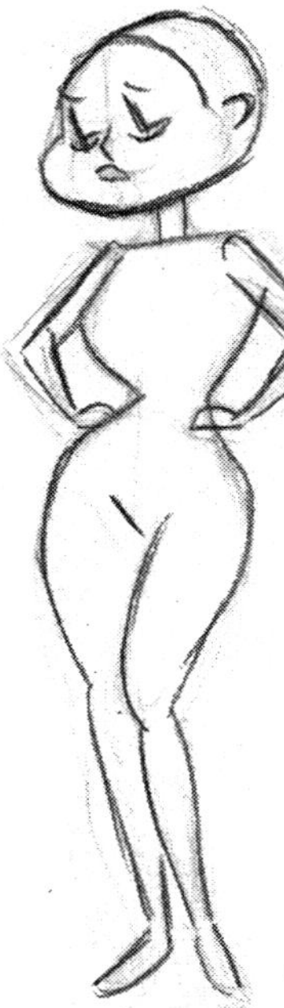

1

2

KEEP IN MIND THAT THESE FIGURES ARE HARDLY THE NORM IN CARTOONING. THERE ARE TOO MANY FAMOUS CARTOON LADIES THAT DON'T MATCH THESE MEASUREMENTS TO LIST HERE. STILL, I THINK IT'S SAFE TO SAY THAT FAR MORE PEOPLE KNOW WHO *MARGE SIMPSON* IS THAN HAVE HEARD OF *JESSICA RABBIT*!

3

NOW LET'S TAKE A LOOK AT THE MALE BODY AND SEE SOME THE WAYS WE CAN TURN IT INTO A CARTOON.

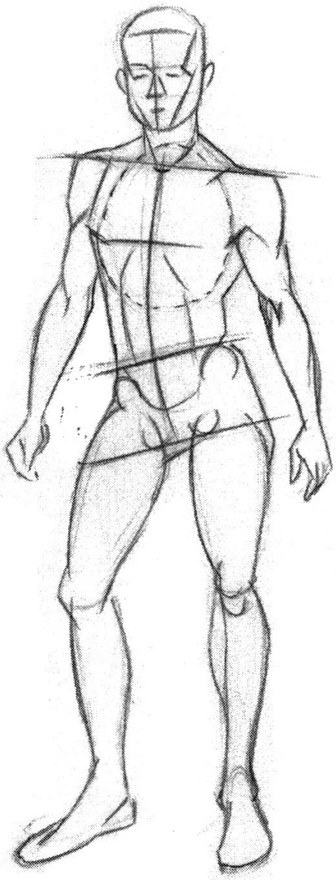

CARTOONING IS ALL ABOUT EXAGGERATION. IN THIS CASE, WE WANT TO MAKE OUR AVERAGE JOE MORE MANLY! MAKE THE SHOULDERS REALLY BROAD AND SHRINK THE WAIST TO MAKE THE UPPER BODY MORE POWERFUL. WE MAY WANT TO SHRINK THE HEAD A LITTLE SO THAT THE BODY SEEMS EVEN BIGGER.

1

2

OF COURSE, WE COULD MAKE HIM LOOK MORE LIKE AN OUT-OF-SHAPE SCHLUB. AN EASY WAY TO DO THAT IS TO TAKE THE LARGER UPPER BODY AND SHIFT IT TO THE LOWER BODY. GIVE HIM A GUT AND NARROW THE WIDTH OF THE SHOULDERS. TOO MANY BURGERS WILL DO THAT TO A GUY!

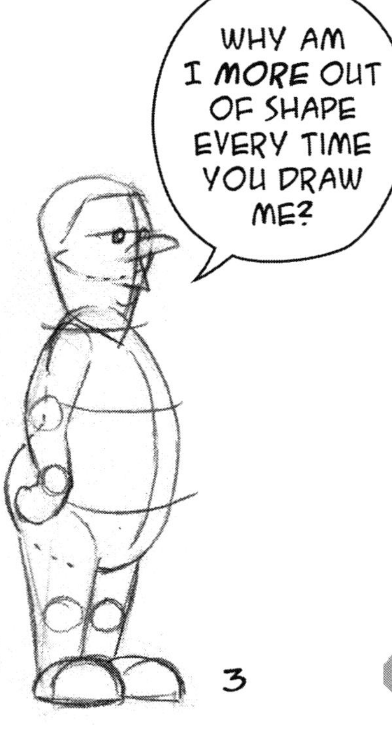

3

DETECTIVE DAWG AND THE SNOOPS

THERE ARE STRANGE THINGS AFOOT AT THE SCHREINENAUF BOARDING SCHOOL. GHOSTS AND MONSTERS ARE HAUNTING ITS HALLS. FORTUNATELY FOR EVERYBODY, ***DORFF,*** THE FAMOUS (AND PUDGY) DETECTIVE DOG, AND HIS FRIENDS ***MISSY, ELLIE,*** AND ***BUNK*** ARE ON THE CASE!

WE'LL START BY PLACING THE CHARACTERS IN POSITIONS TO BEST SHOW THEM OFF, WITH DORFF IN THE FOREGROUND AND THE THREE KIDS BEHIND HIM.

WE'RE USING SIMPLE STICK-AND-BALL SKELETONS TO GET THE POSES RIGHT.

NOW WE CAN BUILD UP FAMILIAR SHAPES OVER OUR SKELETONS.

SINCE OUR CARTOON TAKES PLACE IN A BOARDING SCHOOL, THE KIDS ARE GOING TO BE WEARING UNIFORMS. WE ALSO WANT TO KEEP IN MIND THAT DORFF IS BIG AND FAT, SO LETS PUT A BELLY ON HIM.

NOW THAT WE'VE SKETCHED OUT THE DRAWING, LET'S TRY TO GIVE THE ART SOME MORE PERSONALITY.

LET'S GIVE MISSY A MAGNIFYING GLASS AND HAVE ELLIE LOOKING INTO A MAKEUP COMPACT. I ALSO PUT GLASSES ON MISSY TO MAKE HER SEEM MORE BOOKISH.

SINCE DORFF IS A ST. BERNARD, WE'LL GIVE HIM A KEG ATTACHED TO HIS COLLAR, AS THAT'S WHAT THEY'RE FAMOUS FOR.

FOR THE INTERIOR LINES, WE NEED TO MAKE SURE THAT THEY AREN'T AS THICK AS THE CHARACTER OUTLINES, WHILE KEEPING THEM SIMILAR IN STYLE.

KEEPING THE LINE WORK CONSISTENT THROUGHOUT A DRAWING CAN BE DIFFICULT, BUT IT'S WORTH DOING.

IN THE FINAL DRAWING, THERE IS ONE MAJOR CHANGE: DORFF'S ARM IS LOWERED SLIGHTLY, SO THAT WE CAN ACTUALLY SEE THE KEG AROUND HIS NECK. IF THERE'S AN ELEMENT IN YOUR DRAWING THAT YOU FEEL DOESN'T WORK, DON'T BE AFRAID TO ERASE IT AND TRY AGAIN. IT'S ALL IN THE NAME OF BETTER CARTOONS!

KITTY KATTY

MRS. DELGADO HAS BROUGHT KITTY KATTY HOME TO BE A NEW FRIEND FOR HER TWO ADORABLE DOGS, SWEETIEPIE AND MAULER. SHE HOPES THIS NEW FRIEND WILL STICK AROUND LONGER THAN THE OTHERS. SHE ALSO WONDERS WHERE THE OTHERS RAN OFF TO. KITTY KATTY, ON THE OTHER HAND, DOES NOT.

WE'LL HAVE MRS. DELGADO HOLDING KITTY KATTY IN HER ARMS, AS SWEETIEPIE AND MAULER ARE BEHIND HER, GETTING READY TO GIVE THEIR NEW PLAYMATE THE BEATING OF HIS LIFE!

ALL OF THE CHARACTERS IN THIS PIECE WILL HAVE BEAN-SHAPED BODIES EXCEPT FOR KITTY KATTY, WHOM WE'LL MAKE SKINNY TO PLAY UP HOW FRAIL HE IS.

IF YOU'RE NOT FAMILIAR WITH DOGS, GET SOME REFERENCE TO USE WHILE YOU'RE SKETCHING TO SEE THE RIGHT SHAPES TO USE.

KITTY KATTY

NAILING DOWN THE RIGHT SHAPE AND PLACEMENT OF THE CHARACTERS' FEATURES IS WHERE THE REAL THOUGHT GOES INTO A DRAWING LIKE THIS. THE WAY KITTY KATTY AND HIS FRIENDS ARE DESIGNED HELPS TO DESCRIBE THEIR CHARACTERS.

MOST OF THE HEAVY LIFTING WAS DONE IN THE LAST STEP. NOW WE NEED TO MAKE THE LINEWORK A LITTLE CLEARER.

KITTY KATTY

THE CHANGES IN THE LINEWORK ARE DECIDED BY WHERE THE LIGHT IS COMING FROM. THE LINES ARE THICKER IF THEY ARE ON THE UNDERSIDE OF A SHAPE, AWAY FROM THE LIGHT.

CHANGES IN THE THICKNESS OF A LINE ARE USUALLY CALLED "WEIGHT". THIS JUST REFERS TO THE AMOUNT OF PRESSURE THE ARTIST USES WHEN DRAWING A LINE.

KITTY KATTY

WE'LL USE A BRUSH PEN TO INK THE OUTER LINES. IT'S EASIER TO CREATE THE PROPER LINE WEIGHT USING A BRUSH, SINCE WE DON'T HAVE TO GO OVER THE SAME LINE MULTIPLE TIMES.

WE CAN USE A BRUSH PEN TO INK THE INTERIORS AS WELL. A BRUSH CAN BE A VERY VERSATILE TOOL!

ONCE WE'RE DONE, WE FILL IN ANY BLACK AREAS AND CLEAN UP ANY ROUGH LINES OR MISTAKES WITH WHITE CORRECTION FLUID. THERE ARE DIFFERENT TYPES OF CORRECTION FLUID, SO YOU HAVE TO TEST THEM OUT TO FIND THE ONE THAT WORKS BEST FOR YOU.

MAD MELISSA AND EEEGOR

THERE'S A HOUSE ON GRIMM STREET WHERE STRANGE THINGS ARE HAPPENING. GRANDMOTHER IS BACK FROM THE GRAVE AND HAPPILY BAKING BROWNIES, GARDEN PESTS ARE BEING EATEN ALIVE BY THE GARDEN...AND THEN THERE'S THE CAT. ALL OF THESE HAPPENINGS HAVE ONE PERSON IN COMMON: THE FAMILY'S ELDEST DAUGHTER, MELISSA.

THERE WILL BE FOUR CHARACTERS IN THIS DRAWING: DEAD GRANDMA, FRANKENKITTY, EEEGOR, AND MAD MELISSA (IN THE FOREGROUND).

THESE CHARACTERS WILL HAVE SHAPES THAT AREE MORE DYNAMIC. I'M USING AN ARRAY OF GEOMETRICAL SHAPES TO DEFINE OUR CHARACTERS, NOT JUST CIRCLES AND LINES. FOR THIS STYLE, YOU CAN EXPERIMENT WITH ANY COMBINATION OF GEOMETRIC SHAPES YOU'D LIKE. SEE WHAT WORKS FOR YOUR IDEA!

LET'S CONTINUE TO CREATE OUR DESIGNS BY BUILDING ON THE STRUCTURE WE'VE ALREADY MADE.

AS WE REFINE THE LINE DRAWING, LET'S ADD SOME DETAILS TO GRANDMA. WE PUT SOME DESIGNS ON HER TO INDICATE SHE'S COVERED IN DIRT (SHE *IS* FRESH FROM THE GRAVE), AND A COUPLE OF FLIES BUZZING AROUND HER TO SHOW SHE'S ROTTING.

MAD MELISSA AND EEEGOR

AS WITH THE PREVIOUS EXAMPLES, WE'RE GOING MAKE THE OUTLINES A LITTLE BOLDER IN ORDER TO TIE THE CHARACTERS TOGETHER BETTER.

MAD MELISSA AND EEEGOR

THE INNER LINE ART NEEDS TO BE THIN TO BALANCE WITH THE OUTLINES BETTER. WE DON'T WANT THE LINES TO BLEND WITH ONE ANOTHER.

MAD MELISSA AND EEEGOR

WE'RE INKING THIS WITH A BRUSH PEN JUST TO GIVE A LITTLE SNAP TO THE LINES AND KEEP THEM FROM LOOKING TOO STIFF. GET IT? STIFF? BECAUSE THEY'RE THE LIVING DEAD...NEVER MIND.

HERC AND HIS BROTHERS, ROMAN AND BETO, LOVE TO PLAY THEIR FAVORITE RPG, "THE WARRIORS". OF COURSE, THEY WOULD LOVE IT MORE IF THEIR CAT WOULD STOP RUINING THEIR ADVENTURES BY HOPPING ON THEIR GAME BOARD AND KNOCKING OVER THE MINIATURES, BEGGING FOR ATTENTION IN THE MIDDLE OF A CRUCIAL BATTLE, OR TURNING INTO A TWENTY-FOOT-TALL CAT-DRAGON AND TRYING TO EAT ONE OR MORE OF THEM ALIVE.

YOU MIGHT NOTICE THAT THE ARRANGEMENT OF THE MAIN CHARACTERSS HEADS FORMS A TRIANGLE. BASIC SHAPES CAN BE USED TO HELP US PLACE CHARACTERS IN AN IMAGE, AS WELL AS DRAW THEM!

THE WARRIORS

FOR PROPS, WE'LL HAVE A ROMAN HELMET AND A SWORD FOR ROMAN, A VIKING HELMET AND AXE FOR BETO, AND A BEAR HAT AND CLUB FOR HERC.

IN OUR FINAL DESIGN, BETO GETS SOME HAIR AND FRECKLES, WHILE ROMAN HAS A LARGER PAIR OF LIPS AND A LITTLE STUBBLE ON HIS CHIN.

WE CAN FIND ANY REFERENCE WE NEED TO HELP US DESIGN HELMETS FOR OUR CHARACTERS ONLINE. YOU MAY BE LUCKY ENOUGH TO HAVE THE RIGHT KIND OF REF AT HAND. IF NOT, FIRE UP YOUR COMPUTER AND START SEARCHING!

THE STYLE WE'RE WORKING WITH HERE WOULD LOOK BEST WITH COLOR. THE LARGE OPEN AREAS CRY OUT FOR SOME BOLD COLORS!

A BRUSH WOULDN'T BE A GOOD CHOICE FOR INKING A DRAWING LIKE THIS. THERE ISN'T MUCH CHANGE IN THE THICKNESS OF THE LINES, AND THAT IS WHAT BRUSHES ARE GREAT FOR SHOWING.

HERE'S THE FINAL ART! AGAIN, THERE ISN'T MUCH CHANGE TO THE THICKNESS OF THE LINES, BUT THAT'S NOT WHERE THE FUN IN THE DRAWING COMES FROM. IT'S IN THE STRANGE DESIGNS AND WEIRD FACES!

THE DOINKS

POOR PROFESSOR PEPPERO. HE WENT DOINKING TO UNDOINK THE SECRETS OF THE UNIVERSE, AND INSTEAD UNLEASHED FOUR MISCHIEVOUS DOINKS, WHO ONLY EVER SAY "DOINK", ON THE CITY. WITH ALL OF THE TIME THE PROFESSOR SPENDS CHASING THE DOINKS AROUND AND STOPPING THEM FROM DOINKING ANOTHER DISASTER, HE'S NOT GOING TO HAVE A LOT OF TIME TO DOINKITY DERPY DINKY DOINK!

THIS STYLE USES BEAN SHAPES TO GIVE US THE FORMS OF THE BODIES, AND THE WAY A BODY IS CURVED SHOWS THE CHARACTER'S LINE OF ACTION.

NOW LET'S BUILD UP OUR CHARACTERS ON THE BASIC SHAPES WE'VE MADE. YOU MIGHT HAVE NOTICED THE WAY THE CHARACTERS OVERLAP. THIS OVERLAP WILL HELP GUIDE THE EYE SMOOTHLY THROUGH THE DRAWING.

LET'S GIVE THE PROFESSOR A LAB COAT AND A BOW TIE. HE ALSO GETS SOME WISPS OF HAIR. WE NEED TO CHANGE THE SHAPE OF THE HILL FROM A HALF-CIRCLE TO A HILL WITH A DIP IN IT. THE TREES AND BUILDINGS ARE LEFT FOR THE BACKGROUND.

WITH THAT DONE, LET'S GO OVER THE DRAWING AND MAKE THE LINES A LITTLE CLEARER. WE DON'T WANT TO GET CONFUSED WHILE FINISHING OUR DRAWING.

IN FINISHING UP OUR DRAWING OF THE DOINKS, THE GOAL HERE IS TO MAKE IT CLEAR THAT THE DOINKS ARE REALLY SMALL. ONE WAY TO DO THAT IS BY PLACING THE PROFESSOR BEHIND THE HILL AND THE DOINKS RIGHT UP FRONT!

WE HAVE SOME OPTIONS FOR INKING THIS PIECE. WE COULD USE A BRUSH OR A PEN. FOR THIS DRAWING, A BRUSH WORKS WELL, GIVING A SOFT, SMOOTH FEEL TO THE LINES.

HERE'S THE FINISHED PIECE! WE USED A PEN FOR SOME OF THE FINE DETAILS, LIKE THE PROFESSOR'S FACE.

NOW THE PROFESSOR AND THE DOINKS CAN DOINKY DINK AND DERP DOINKITY DOINK!

PRESTO-DIGITAL LABS HAS A SECRET WEAPON THAT ALLOWS THEM TO MAKE INCREDIBLE DISCOVERIES AND BE VERY PROFITABLE. ACTUALLY THEY HAVE THREE: THREE GENETICALLY ENHANCED LAB MICE NAMED CARL, STEVE AND BERT. THE THREE MICE SPEND THEIR DAYS SPLITTING ATOMS, CREATING NEW, CUTTING-EDGE TECHNOLOGIES, AND NEARLY DESTROYING THE WORLD. ALL IN A DAY'S WORK WHEN YOU'RE A TRIO OF SUPER-GENIUS MICE.

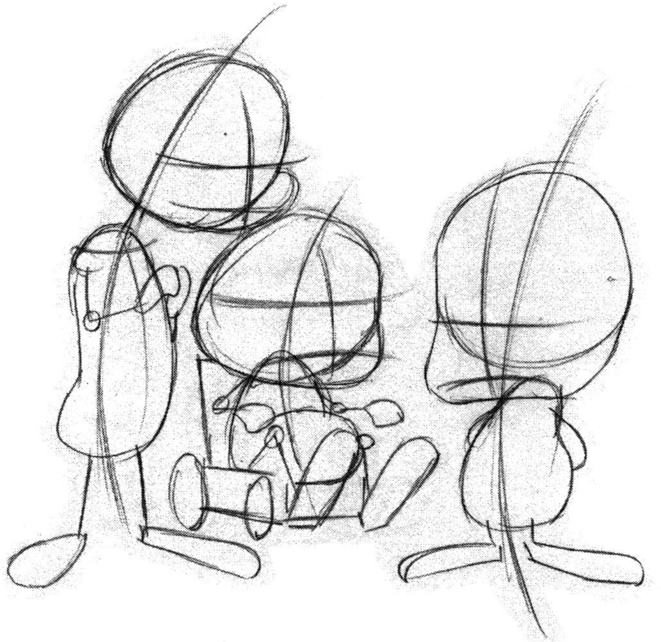

LET'S SKETCH IN OUR BASIC FIGURES. WE'VE GIVEN THE MICE DIFFERENT HEAD-TO-BODY SIZES TO PLAY WITH THE HEIGHT OF EACH ONE.

NOW WE CAN DESIGN OUR MICE! EACH MOUSE NEEDS TO BRING DIFFERENT VISUAL ELEMENTS TO THE DRAWING THAT MAKE IT CLEAR WHO IS WHO, SO EACH HAS HIS OWN HEAD SHAPE, HAIRSTYLE, AND CLOTHES! ONE OF THE MICE EVEN GETS A MOTORIZED CHAIR!

HERE'S OUR PENCILLED ART. WE'VE ADDED SOME LINE WEIGHT TO THE PENCILS, JUST TO GIVE THEM A LITTLE MORE STYLE. THIS IS GOOD ENOUGH FOR MOST ARTISTS, BUT WE'RE GOING TO GO FURTHER AND INK OUR PENCILS!

WE'RE GOING TO INK OUR MICE WITH A BRUSH. HERE WE'VE DONE THE OUTLINES FIRST, BUT YOU COULD INK EACH MOUSE ONE AT A TIME. THIS APPROACH JUST KEEPS THINGS A LITTLE MORE ORDERLY.

AS YOU CAN SEE, WE'VE FOLLOWED THE PENCILS PRETTY CLOSELY. IF YOU'RE INKING YOUR OWN ART, THEN YOU DON'T HAVE TO PENCIL THE ART AS TIGHTLY AS WE DID HERE.

HORSEFLIERS

JUMPER AND NAY SPEND THEIR DAYS IN THE MAGICAL RAINFOREST OF NUGMEE, MEETING NEW FRIENDS, EATING DELICIOUS FRUIT, AND USING THEIR MAGICAL WINGS TO SOAR THROUGH THE CLOUDS. AHH...IT'S A HORSE'S LIFE.

DRAWING HORSES CAN BE REALLY EASY, ESPECIALLY WITH THE PRACTICE WE'VE HAD DRAWING CHARACTERS BY THIS POINT! WE'RE JUST GOING TO APPLY WHAT WE'VE LEARNED ABOUT USING SHAPES TO BUILD AND DESIGN OUR DRAWINGS.

NOW WE CAN BUILD UP THE FEATURES FOR JUMPER AND NAY, AS WE'VE DONE IN OUR OTHER EXAMPLES.

LET'S GO AHEAD AND TIGHTEN THE PENCIL LINES, JUST TO MAKE THINGS CLEARER AND EASIER TO UNDERSTAND.

MAKING THE LINE WORK A LITTLE BOLDER WILL HELP OUR DRAW TO POP OFF OF THE PAGE BETTER.

HORSEFLIERS

WE'RE LOOKING FOR REALLY SMOOTH LINES TO PULL OFF THE LOOK WE WANT. A REALLY STEADY HAND AND BEING ABLE TO PAY CLOSE ATTENTION TO THE LINES ARE WHAT WE NEED MOST!

VISUAL VOCABULARY

KEEPING IT SIMPLE!

DON'T OVER-THINK DESIGNS LIKE THIS! TOO OFTEN, ARTISTS BUILD UNNECESSARY FORMS AND SHAPES THAT JUST DON'T BELONG. AIM FOR BASIC SHAPES THAT WORK WELL TOGETHER. OTHERWISE, YOU'RE GOING TO END UP WITH UGLY, CLUNKY DESIGNS, AND NOBODY WANTS THAT!

CHEEZE AND QUACKERS

FINDING A JOB IN THE BIG CITY IS HARD ENOUGH. WHEN YOU'RE COMPETING FOR EVERY JOB WITH A NUTTY DUCK WHO'S READY TO PULL EVERY DIRTY TRICK A 'TOON CAN THINK UP TO GET AHEAD, IT GETS MUCH HARDER. BUT IF YOU'RE A RASCALLY RODENT, YOU'VE ALWAYS GOT A FEW TRICKS UP YOUR SLEEVES!

LET'S LAY DOWN THE BASIC SHAPES FOR OUR DUCK AND RAT CHARACTERS. WE NEED TO KEEP THE SHAPES PRETTY BASIC, SINCE WE WANT TO KNOW WHO THE CHARACTERS ARE EVEN IN SILHOUETTE!

IT WOULD BE COOL TO SHOW THESE GUYS GOING AT EACH OTHER WITH HAMMERS AND ANVILS, OR EVEN DYNAMITE! WE'RE JUST DESIGNING THEM RIGHT NOW, THOUGH, SO MAYBE WE CAN DO THAT LATER.

AS WE COMPLETE THE DESIGN, QUACKERS GETS A BOW TIE AND SOME FEATHERS ON HIS HEAD. LET'S MAKE SURE YOU CAN TELL CHEEZE IS WEARING A HAT.

LET'S GO OVER THE LINES ONE MORE TIME, JUST TO GIVE THEM A LITTLE MORE PERSONALITY!

OKAY, PENCILS ARE DONE, LET'S START INKING!

HERE IS THE FINAL DRAWING! WHY DON'T WE SEE WHAT THESE GUYS LOOK LIKE IN ACTION?

THAT'S PRETTY GOOD! THESE GUYS WILL DO ANYTHING FOR A JOB!
U.S. ANVIL CO.

PEST BUDS

BUZZ AND SCRATCH HAVE KNOWN EACH OTHER SINCE THEY WERE LARVAE GROWING UP TOGETHER ON A BANANA PEEL. NOW THEY'RE YOUNG FLIES, OUT ON THEIR OWN, MAKING THEIR WAY AROUND THE CRAZY WORLD OF MRS. KITHEN'S KITCHEN AND TRYING NOT TO GET SWATTED OR SPRAYED AS THEY LEARN WHAT LIFE'S ABOUT.

AS WE'VE DONE BEFORE, WE COMPOSE THE CHARACTERS AND MAJOR BACKGROUND ELEMENT TO GUIDE THE EYE. THIS TIME, WE BRING IT IN A SPIRAL. DOING THIS MAKES SURE THE VIEWER AUTOMATICALLY TAKES IN EVERYTHING IMPORTANT.

NEXT, LET'S GIVE BUZZ AND SCRATCH WINGS AND ANTENNAE, AND PUT THE LINES FOR BUZZ'S T-SHIRT ON HIM. WE ALSO START DESIGNING THE LABEL FOR THE CAN OF BUG SPRAY, NOTING WHERE THE LETTERS AND SHAPES WILL BE.

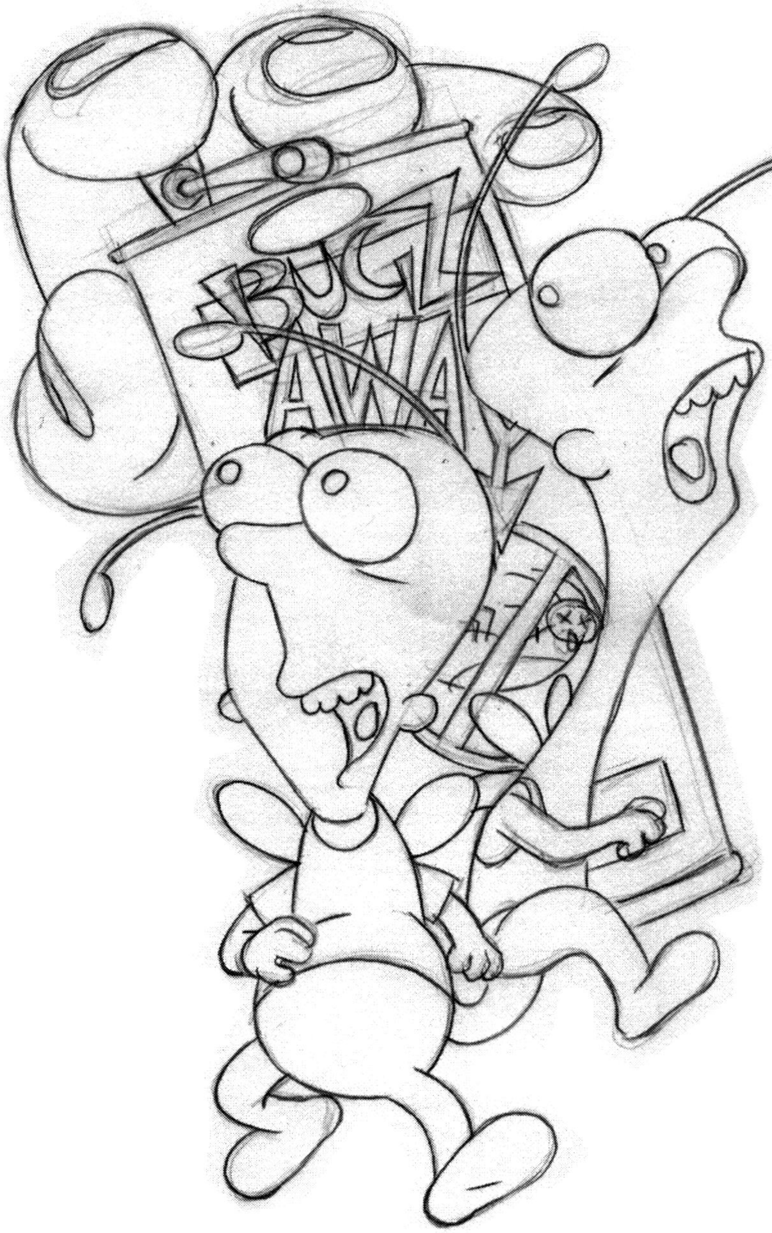

IN OUR FINAL PENCILS, WE'VE STRENGTHENED THE LINES, BUT WE'RE NOT MAKING THEM TOO BOLD. IF THE LINES ARE TOO THICK, THEY COULD START TO CLUTTER THE ART AND MAKE IT HARD TO READ.

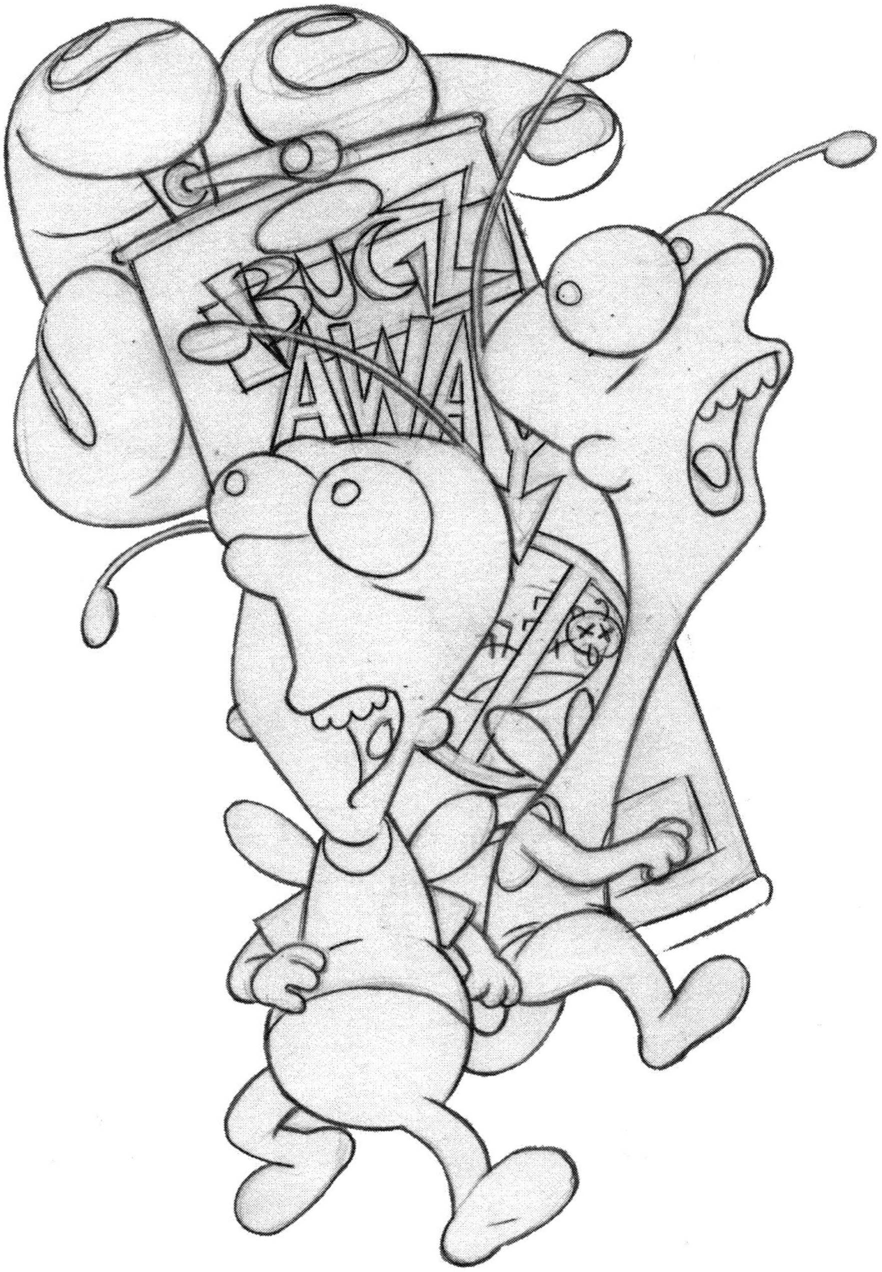

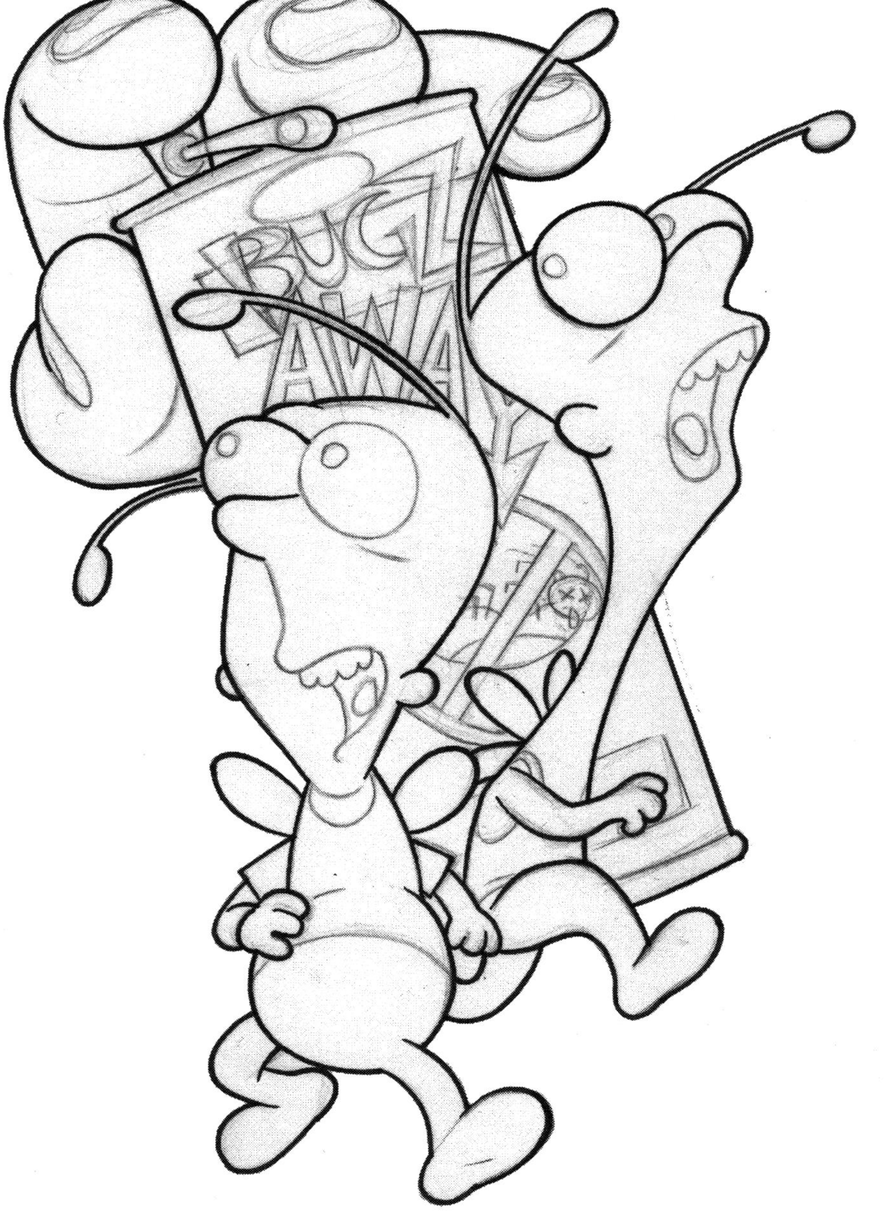

LET'S START THE INKS! YOU DON'T HAVE TO INK YOUR DRAWINGS, OF COURSE. IN FACT, MANY PEOPLE TEND TO LIKE THEIR PENCILS FAR BETTER THAN THEIR INKS!

WE'LL CARRY THOSE THOUGHTS OVER TO THE INKS. IT'S A LITTLE HARD TO DRAW LIKE THIS AND KEEP THE ART LOOKING LIVELY. TRY TO PRACTICE AND SEE IF A STYLE LIKE THIS WORKS FOR YOU!

WE KNOW A LOT OF PEOPLE WHO SAY THAT THEIR BOSS IS A MONSTER. AT THE MONSTERMART, NOT ONLY IS THE BOSS REALLY MONSTER, EVERYONE IS! BERNIE AND HIS BUDDY EARL ARE JUST TRYING TO GET THROUGH WORK DAY WITHOUT DRAWING THE IRE OF THEIR BOSS, MISTER JOWLS, WHOSE IDEA OF TERMINATION IS EATING YOU FOR LUNCH!

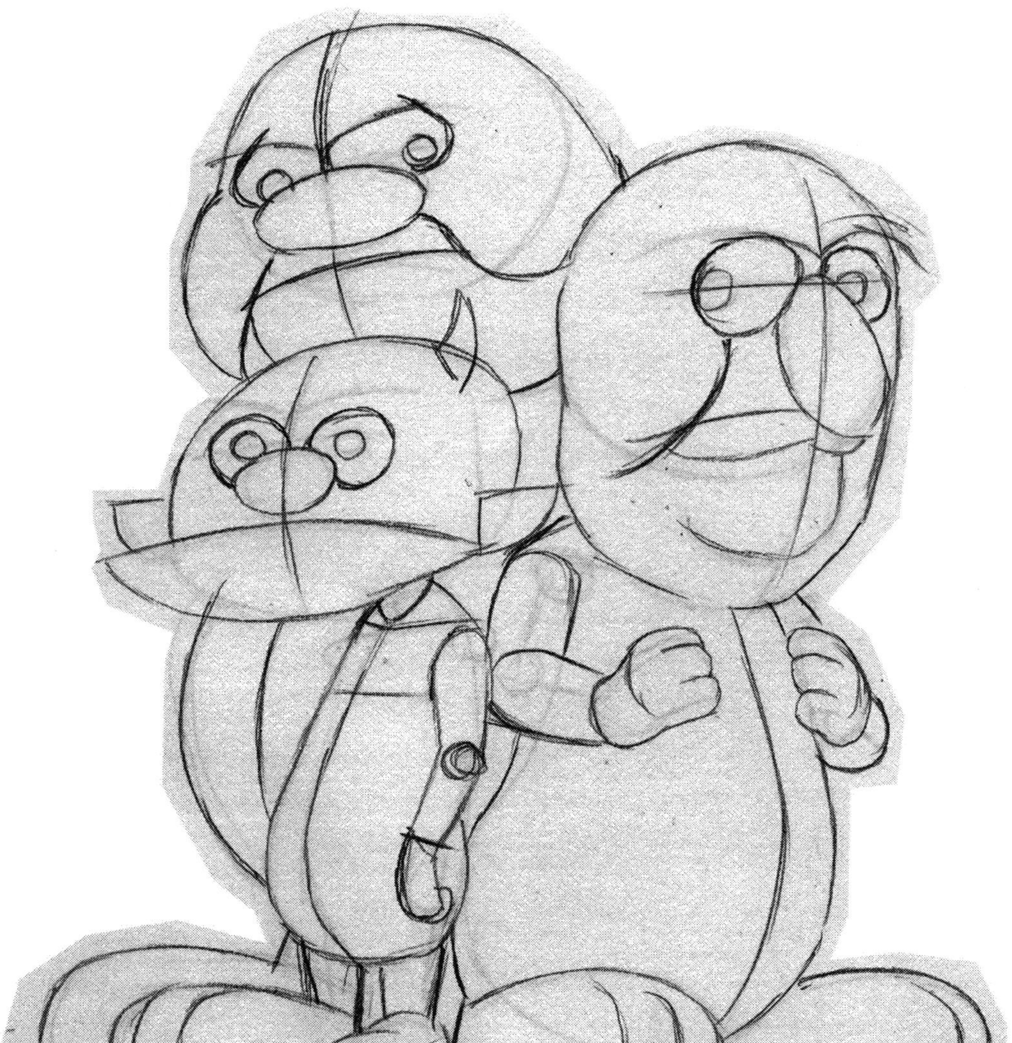

LET'S LAY DOWN SOME BASIC SHAPES FOR SOME PROPERLY MONSTROUS FIGURES!

THE HAIR FOR THESE CHARACTERS HAS A MORE FEATHERY SHAPE THAN NORMAL FUR. IT JUST SEEMS A LITTLE NICER-LOOKING.

TO FINISH OFF THE LINEWORK, WE'RE GOING TO GO OVER THE LINES IN A STYLE WE'VE USED IN SOME OF OUR OTHER EXAMPLES.

WE SHOULD GO AHEAD AND INK OUR DRAWING, BUT THERE'S A PROBLEM: WE NEED TO CHANGE THE DESIGN OF THE BOSS. HE'S JUST TOO SMALL, AND HE'S BLOCKED FROM OUR VIEW. NOT ONLY THAT, BUT HE LOOKS TOO MUCH LIKE BERNIE AND EARL.

LET'S STOP RIGHT HERE AND REWORK OUR BOSS CHARACTER, AND WE'LL CONTINUE ON THE NEXT PAGE!

WE THINK THIS WORKS BETTER; THE BOSS IS A LOT LARGER THAN HIS WORKERS, AND HIS LOOK SETS HIM APART FROM THE OTHERS. (OF COURSE, WE PROBABLY CAN'T CALL HIM MR. JOWLS NOW...) WHAT DO YOU THINK?

THE HISTOCRATS

WHEN JULIUS CAESAR AND NAPOLEON BONAPARTE ARE EXILED FROM THEIR RESPECTIVE COUNTRIES, WHAT ARE TWO EX-DICTATORS TO DO? GET AN APARTMENT TOGETHER IN THE BIG CITY, OF COURSE! THERE ARE LOTS OF FOLKS WHO SAY THEY HAVE A TYRANT FOR A ROOMMATE, BUT THESE GUYS ARE THE REAL DEAL!

LET'S START BY PUTTING OUR CHARACTERS IN POSES THAT WE MIGHT EXPECT TO SEE THEM USING: NAPOLEON WITH HIS HAND INSIDE HIS COAT, AND CAESAR GESTURING AS IF GIVING A SPEECH.

AS WE PENCIL OUT THE FINAL DESIGN, LET'S MAKE SURE WE HAVE THE RIGHT ATTITUDE ON THE CHARACTERS' FACES. NAPOLEON IS SNOBBY, AND CAESAR IS A GOOD-NATURED FAST-TALKER.

WE'LL GIVE OUR HISTOCRATS NICE, BOLD LINES, SO THAT THEY READ A LITTLE MORE CLEARLY. AS WE OUTLINE THE CHARACTERS, WE WORK ON DEFINING THE HANDS AND FEET A LITTLE MORE ON BOTH OF THEM TO MAKE THEM LOOK MORE SOLID. REMEMBER, IT'S NEVER TOO LATE TO FIX A MISTAKE!

OKAY, LET'S GET IN THERE AND START INKING! WOW, THE CHARACTERS ALREADY POP ON THE PAGE!

THE INNER LINES ARE GOING TO BE A LOT THINNER THAN THE OUTLINES. AS WE INK, WE NEED TO GIVE THE LINES A LITTLE "SNAP" TO PROVIDE THEM SOME EXTRA LIFE!

H.U.B. IS A MAJOR METROPOLITAN CITY IN THE GRIP OF CRIMINALS AND TERRORISTS. FORTUNATELY FOR THE PEOPLE, THE MYSTERIOUS VIGILANTE KNOWN AS INDIGHOST IS ALWAYS ON THE CASE. TO SOME, HE'S A HERO, TO OTHERS, A MENACE. BUT TO THE UNDERWORLD OF CRIME, HE'S THEIR WORST NIGHTMARE!

FOR THIS DRAWING, LET'S INCLUDE INDIGHOST'S GREATEST ENEMIES, DR. SURGIKILL AND BLOODRED DEAD. A GOOD HERO NEEDS SOME COOL-LOOKING VILLAINS TO BATTLE!

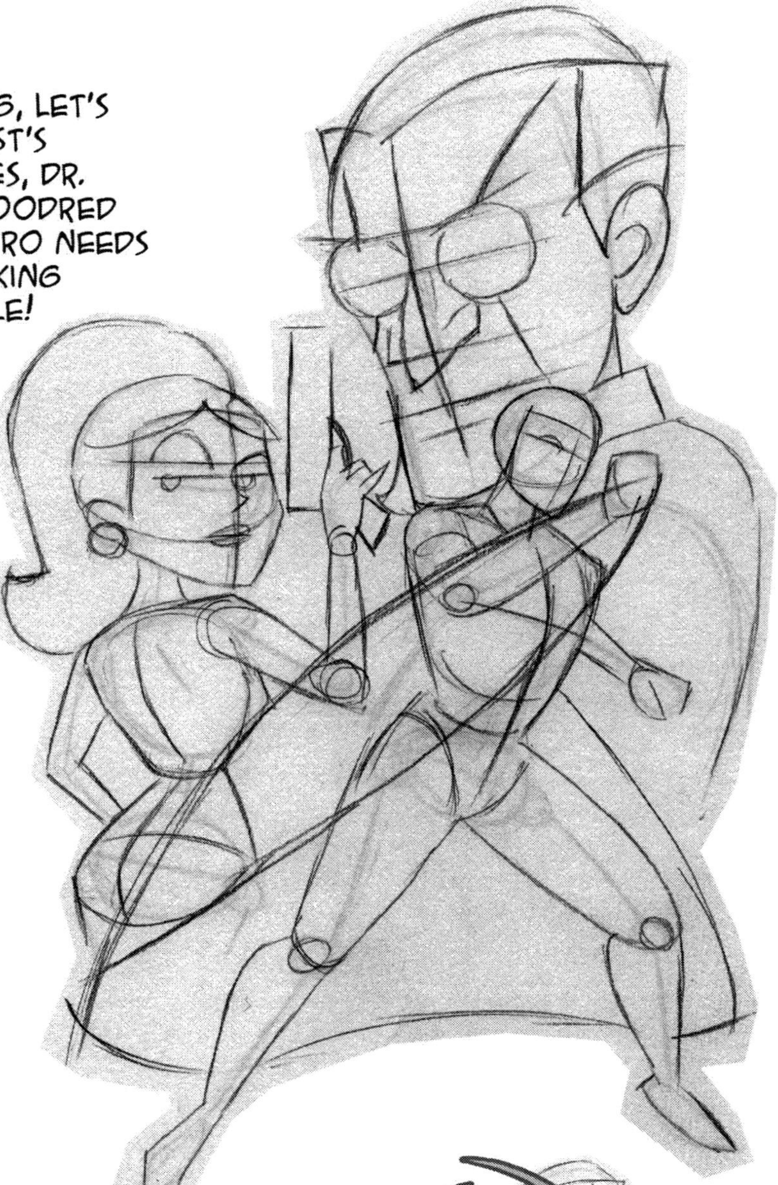

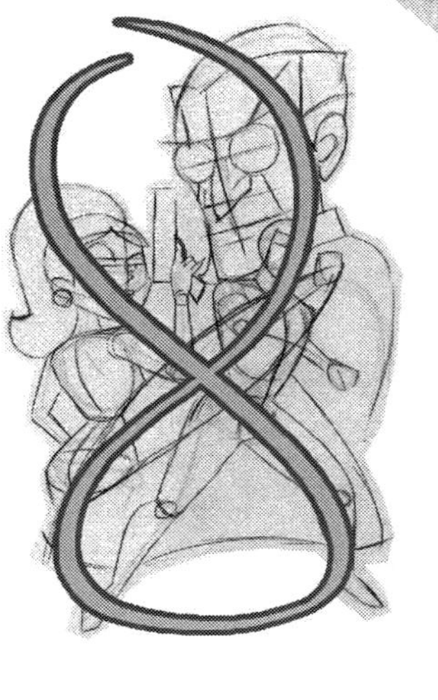

HMM..THERE'S AN INTERESTING FIGURE-EIGHT FLOW TO THE DESIGN. CAN YOU SEE IT?

AS WE DESIGN THE CHARACTERS, WE KEEP EVERYTHING SIMPLE. THE HERO GETS A COWL, A COLLAR, AND A BELT WITH TWO CAPSULES ON EITHER SIDE OF THE ROUND BUCKLE. BLOODRED DEAD GETS A SKULL PAINTED ON HER FACE, A BELT, NECKLACE AND EARRINGS, AND A GUN THAT'S SLIGHTLY MORE DETAILED. FOR DR. SURGIKILL, WE JUST CONTINUE WHAT WE STARTED IN THE LAST STEP.

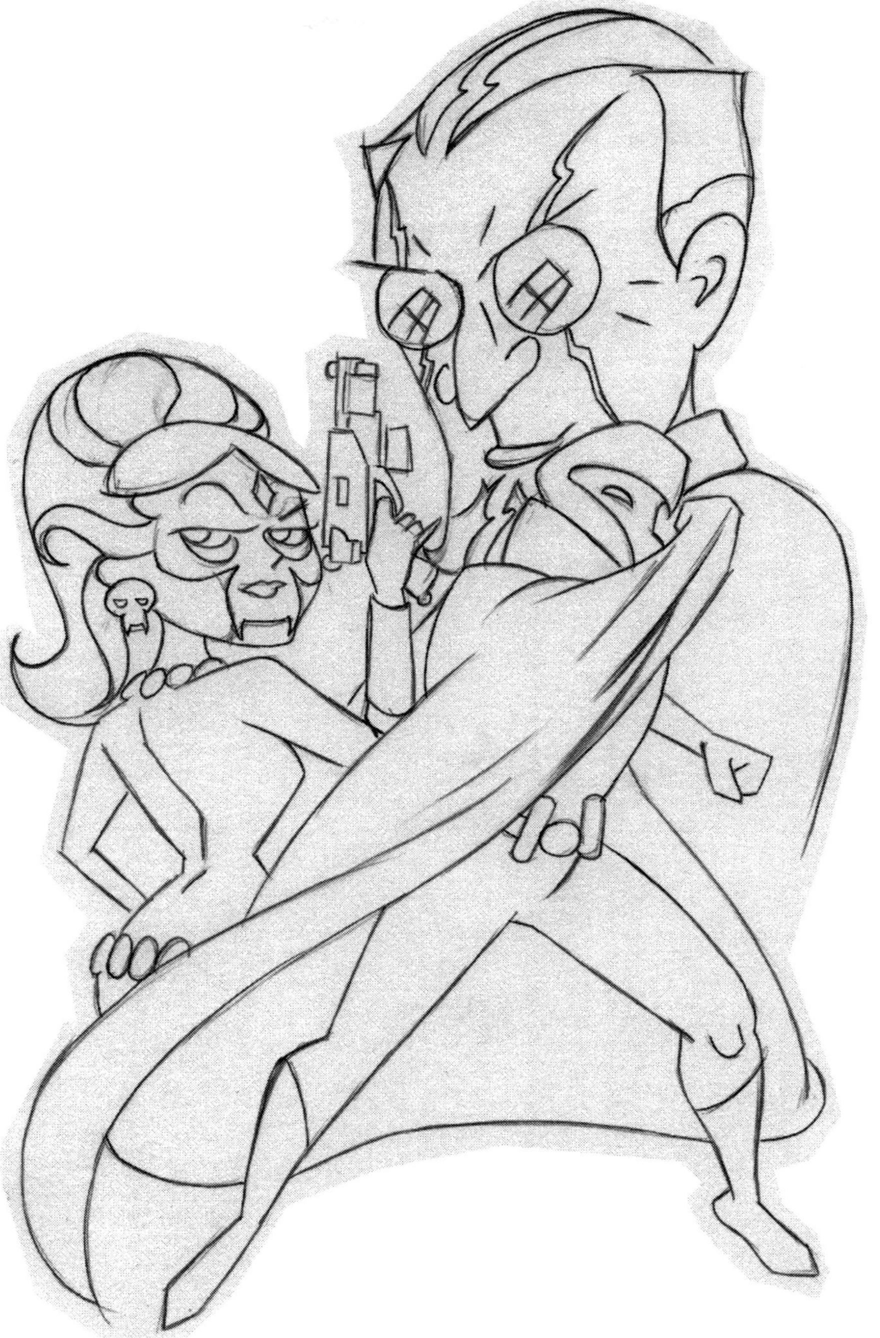

FOR OUR FINAL DESIGN, WE SIMPLIFY INDIGHOST'S CAPE AND DECIDE TO GIVE HIM BOOTS. FOR BLOODRED DEAD, WE CAN REFINE HER HAIR, JEWELRY AND GUN, AND GIVE HER A BRACELET. DOKTOR SURGIKILL'S SCARS ARE MORE DEFINED, AND WE'LL PUT SOME PATTERNS IN HIS HAIR.

FOR THIS STEP, WE'RE GOING TO ADD SOME THICKNESS TO THE OUTLINES TO MAKE OUR CHARACTERS EVEN MORE STYLISH!

AS WE INK OUR HERO AND VILLAINS, LET'S MAKE SURE THE LINES HAVE ENOUGH VARIATION TO MAKE THEM INTERESTING.

IN THE FINISHED DRAWING, WE'VE MANAGED TO KEEP THE CARTOONISH FEEL. FILLING THE INSIDE OF THE CAPE WITH SOLID BLACK IS A GOOD IDEA, SINCE IT HELPS TO POP OUT INDIGHOST'S BODY.

RY-BOT

RYAN FRANK SAYS HE'S JUST ANOTHER GUY ATTENDING COLLEGE IN SUNNY CALIFORNIA. IN TRUTH, RYAN IS AN UNDERCOVER AGENT FROM SPACE! HE'S ON EARTH TRACKING DOWN A GROUP OF DESPERATE ALIENS HIDING IN THE LOCAL POPULATION. ARMED WITH HIS I-ARMOR AND HIS ANDROID CAT, ALBERT, RYAN IS READY TO DISPENSE GALACTIC-SIZED JUSTICE ON PLANET EARTH!

AS WE START TO BUILD UP THE BODY SHAPES, WE GET RIGHT INTO DESIGNING RYAN'S I-ARMOR SHAPES, WHAT RYAN'S HAIR WILL LOOK LIKE, AND THE BASIC LOOK OF ALBERT.

MOVING AHEAD WITH THE DESIGN, LET'S ADD SOME CLOTHING SHAPES TO RYAN, PUT INTERIOR LINES ON THE I-ARMOR, AND CLEAN UP ALBERT'S DESIGN.

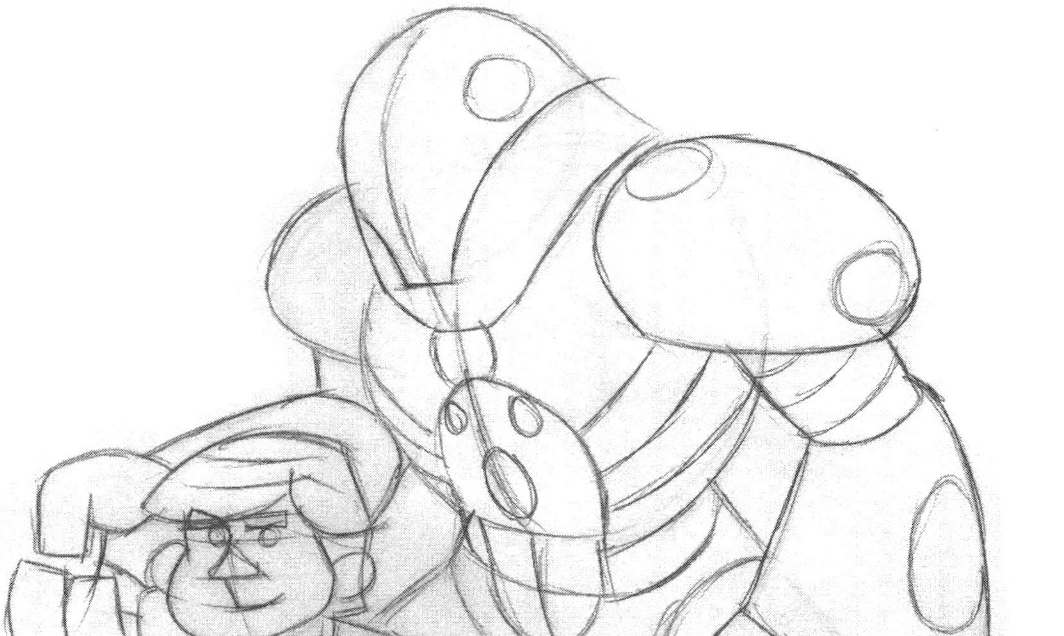

IN OUR FINAL DESIGN, LET'S ADD THE LETTERING AND STRIPES TO RYAN'S JERSEY, FINISH THE INTERIOR LINES OF THE I-ARMOR, AND ADD SOME DETAIL TO ALBERT'S FUR AND EYES.

RY-BOT

THE PENCIL LINES NEED TO BE STRONG AND SLEEK TO HELP MAKE THE ART LOOK A LITTLE MORE ACTION-PACKED!

THE INSIDE LINES OF THE CHARACTERS ARE GOING TO BE THINNER THAN THE OUTLINES SO THAT THE CHARCTERS DON'T BLEND TOGETHER.

AS WE INK IN THE CHARACTERS, RYAN AND ALBERT'S DESIGNS WILL GO A LITTLE QUICKER. THEIR DESIGNS DON'T HAVE TO BE TOO EXACT, WHILE THE I-ARMOR IS A ROBOT, SO IT NEEDS TO LOOK MORE LIKE A MACHINE TO BE CONVINCING.

HERE'S OUR FINAL ART! DRAWING ROBOTS CAN BE TIME-CONSUMING, AND IT MAY REQUIRE A LOT OF REFERENCE, BUT IT'S WORTH IT!

THE SWORD OF TY-TAN

IN A DISTANT GALAXY, THE EVIL OVERLORD OSSEUS CONTROLS HIS EMPIRE THROUGH THE USE OF HIS MAGICAL SCIENCE! ONE MAN STANDS IN HIS WAY: JAAN ZAMM, WIELDER OF THE MAGICAL SWORD OF TY-TAN! JAAN AND HIS BAND OF FREEDOM FIGHTERS TRAVEL FROM WORLD TO WORLD ON A MISSION TO RESCUE THE GALAXY FROM OSSEUS AND HIS MINIONS!

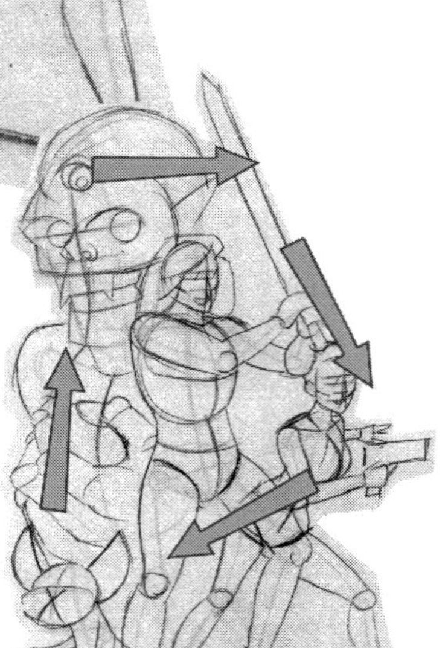

ONCE AGAIN, WE'RE TRYING TO GUIDE THE EYE AROUND THE PAGE WITH INTERESTING ANGLES AND IMAGES. WE LEAD FROM OSSEUS' EYE TO THE SWORD TO THE BLASTER TO THE ANIMAL AND BACK AGAIN!

WE'RE GOING TO BE DRAWING MORE REALISTIC CHARACTERS THIS TIME. IF YOU'RE NOT COMFORTABLE WITH THESE KINDS OF FIGURES, FIND SOME REFERENCE AS A GUIDE. YOU COULD EVEN GET YOUR FRIENDS TO POSE FOR YOU WHEN YOU NEED A UNIQUE POSE.

THE SWORD OF TY-TAN

EVEN THOUGH WE'RE GOING FOR A REALISTIC STYLE, WE NEED TO KEEP THINGS SIMPLE AND EASY TO UNDERSTAND. TOO MUCH DETAIL CAN MAKE A DRAWING REALLY CONFUSING IF IT ISN'T HANDLED WELL.

AS WE INK OUR DRAWING, LET'S TRY TO KEEP A SKETCHY QUALITY TO THE LINES, BUT WE'LL MAKE SURE THAT THEY DON'T LOOK RUSHED IN THE PROCESS.

THERE WE GO! OUR HEROES LOOK HEROIC, OSSEUS LOOKS REALLY CREEPY...AND MAYBE JAAN'S PET CAME OUT EVEN CREEPIER?

WE HOPE YOU WERE ABLE TO GET A LOT OF USEFUL INFO OUT OF THESE EXAMPLES! KEEP DRAWING, AND WE'LL SEE YOU AGAIN SOON!

BIBLIOGRAPHY

Cartoon Animation by Preston Blair
ISBN: 1-56010-084-2

A great book that teaches aspiring artists how to construct a cartoon character the right way, as well as showing how to best take advantage of the line of action.

The Animator's Survival Kit by Richard Williams
ISBN: 0-57120-228-4

As much an animator's journey as it is an instructional tool, following the exercises and insights from this book will make you a better artist and animator.

Understanding Comics: The Invisible Art by Scott McCloud
ISBN: 0-06-097625-X

This book opens entirely new vistas in the world of art, not just comics. If you don't get this book you are cheating yourself and lessening you knowledge of the mechanics of cartooning.

Batman: Animated by Paul Dini and Chip Kidd
ISBN: 0-06-107327-X

A wonderful artbook, featuring the great art that went into the creation and production of Batman: The Animated Series. Bruce Timm is one of the most important animators of the modern era, and this book shows why.

Comics and Sequential Art by Will Eisner
ISBN: 0-39-333126-1

Written by a comics pioneer, the language of cartooning is brought to life and explained in a clear, understandable way for artists of any level of experience.